the allotment gardener

Ann Nicol

the *allotment*
gardener

Published by SILVERDALE BOOKS
An imprint of Bookmart Ltd
Registered number 2372865
Trading as Bookmart Ltd
Blaby Road
Wigston
Leicester LE18 4SE

© 2006 D&S Books Ltd

D&S Books Ltd
Kerswell,
Parkham Ash, Bideford
Devon, England
EX39 5PR

e-mail us at:- enquiries@d-sbooks.co.uk

This edition printed 2007

ISBN 13: 9-781-84509-292-4

DS0109. Allotment Gardener

Creative Director: Sarah King
Editor: Anna Southgate
Project Editor: Judith Millidge
Photography: Colin Bowling
Designer: Laura Forrester

Printed in Thailand

3 5 7 9 10 8 6 4 2

CONTENTS

INTRODUCTION

For centuries, productive gardens have been the focal point of communities all over the world. Now there is an increased demand for organic and home-grown fruits and vegetables, as many people turn away from commercially grown crops. Luckily, this trend brings benefits to both your health and your pocket. You will find allotment gardening can be an enormously enjoyable leisure activity, and this book will help you grow exactly what you want with confidence.

Until you have grown your own produce, you cannot appreciate what a delight fresh fruit and vegetables are from your own garden, compared to those bought in a shop. The flavour and texture of freshly dug vegetables, or ripe fruits fresh from your plot, are so different from those that have been stored for days. Modern shopping trends mean that we can buy food that has been flown in from all over the world at any time of the year. When you grow your own crops, the harvest is dependant on the seasons and weather in your region and you will appreciate juicy home-grown strawberries ripened in June so much more than those tasteless ones imported in December.

Growing good crops takes time and experience, but the secret of gardening for newcomers is not to be too ambitious and to realise you will see both success and failure in your first year. You will learn from experience and with a little patience, you will soon be producing your own crops with a tremendous feeling of pride and satisfaction.

You may be concerned over the use of chemicals in modern horticultural practice. Growing your own fruit and vegetables means that you will have total control over what goes into the soil and that you will have the opportunity to keep your home-grown produce wholesome and free of chemicals.

When you work an allotment or small plot of land, you will find you share the pleasure of growing with others. Your neighbours will offer advice on the locality, swap knowledge, plants and produce with you and you will be popular with friends when you pass on the odd lettuce or bag of beans. You will find in the natural pattern of growing that there are times of the year when a glut of fruit and vegetables will produce all at the same time – although these are ideal for freezing and preserving.

Gardening is a constant learning process and this book is intended to help guide the reader into first choosing varieties, then working through the basics for planting, growing and harvesting a crop successfully. Each item has practical advice and tips on climate, propagation, pests, weeds and diseases, all designed to give you as much help as possible. There is nothing more satisfying than standing back to admire your plot of land, well stocked with produce. After all your hard work, you will find it well worth the effort.

Happy gardening,

Ann Nicol

HOW TO GROW

THE SOIL

Preparation

First test your soil. Most plants will grow well in ordinary soil, but others will need special nourishment and conditions. You will need to test the soil to see whether it is acid or alkaline. You will also need to find whether it requires any special attention: for instance, clay soil which retains water, will need to be broken down and aerated with compost or grit for plants to grow successfully.

The pH scale is a way of measuring the acid or alkaline content of the soil. Most soils vary between pH6.0, which is slightly acid and pH7.0 which is neutral. An acid soil is one where the pH level is below 7.0 and this soil may be peaty, sandy and light, or heavy clay. An acid soil has a low lime content. Soils high in lime are alkaline. A simple soil test kit will determine the type of soil in your area and can be obtained from garden centres or chemists' shops.

Soil types – and improving them

Soils which have not been cultivated for several years may be deficient in some of the elements needed for good growth and may need improving.

Try to use organic, rather than chemical fertilisers to enrich your soil if it is deficient in any one of the elements needed for good crops.

Calcium deficiency

- *Indicated by black heart in celery, browned centres in Brussels sprouts, tip burn in lettuce, and blossom end rot in tomatoes.*

– Dig in plenty of well rotted manure or organic compost.

TESTING THE CONTENT OF SOIL

Magnesium deficiency
- *Indicated by yellowing of leaves.*

– Apply liquid seaweed or liquid animal manure.

Nitrogen deficiency
- *Indicated by old leaves becoming yellow, young leaves are soft and very green and the plants are stunted.*

– Apply high nitrogen fertiliser such as dried blood.

Phosphorous deficiency
- *Indicated by distinctive blue leaves and stunted growth.*

– Apply bone meal fertiliser.

Potassium deficiency
- *Indicated by stunted plants, bronze leaves, small flowers and fruit.*

– Apply rock potash.

Sulphur deficiency
- *Indicated by stunted growth and yellowing of leaves.*

– Apply a light dusting of calcium sulphate or horticultural gypsum.

Creating rich loam

The plants in your plot need a variety of nutrients for healthy growth to provide vegetables and fruit. In most cases, the soil will need occasional improvement to help it meet these demands. Loam is the name given to a balance of clay, sand and humus, which is the ideal form of soil for growing.

NEGLECTED GROUND

The first job to do on a piece of neglected land, is to remove all trace of weeds and dig over the soil. Remove all the roots as well as the top growth and remember that most weeds will re-grow from a small amount of root left in the soil.

WEEDS WILL FLOURISH ON NEGLECTED LAND.

Soil texture

Dig in material before you plant in spring so that new growth can get off to the best start. Determine what your soil needs. Garden centres and nurseries offer a range of home test kits to check your soil content. Soil problems are corrected by adding natural conditioners and most improve the soil in a number of different ways.

• **Garden compost** is an organic, dark rich crumbly material with a coarse texture. The nutrients will depend on what was composted, but it will always improve soil texture.

• **Composted horse or farmyard manure** – a well-rotted, rich dark textured manure easy to work into the soil and readily available in country areas. Rich in nitrogen, it also improves the drainage and moisture retention in the soil.

• **Builder's sand** – is a coarse natural sand which has larger grains than beach sand. It improves drainage and helps loosen soil, so is ideal for aerating heavy clay soils.

• **Cocoa shell** – this is sold in large bags and is crisp and brown with a rich chocolate aroma. It adds humus and plant food, helps retain moisture and if used as a top dressing, will also keep down weeds.

• **Shredded bark** – can be made from ground bark or wood chippings. This improves soil texture, making it airy and aiding soil drainage.

• **Leaf mould** – easy to make yourself from raked up and composted leaves. It is high in nitrogen and potassium, and these nutrients are slowly released into the soil.

COMPOST.

DIGGING THE PLOT

In most years, it is only necessary to dig the soil to a spade's depth. It is a good idea to dig over more deeply every four to five years to stop a compressed layer from forming which will impair drainage. Digging allows compost to be included at a deeper level, which will encourage roots to grow downward and draw nutrients from a greater depth. Deeper digging helps plants withstand drought and means they can be planted closer together.

HOW TO DIG

Single digging

How thoroughly you need to dig your plot, will depend on your soil type. Start at one end of the plot and dig a trench – a spade's depth. Spread some well-rotted manure along the base of the trench. When you have prepared the first trench, start digging a second alongside the first one. As you break up the soil, pile it into the first trench. Continue to dig and fill in the trenches with compost, then soil.

Double digging

Double digging is done in a similar way to single digging, except that the soil at the base of the trench is loosened to a further spade's depth with a fork. A good layer of manure or compost is put into the bottom of the trench and the

soil from the second trench is spread over the manure in the first and forked to mix together.

Once the soil has been dug over it is important to keep off it. The structure of the soil is easily destroyed, so keep beds to a size that will allow you to attend to plants without walking on the soil. Use a plank to walk on the surface to minimise damage.

Soil aeration

It is vital that the soil should hold air in order to allow essential micro-organisms to breathe. In some soils, particularly clay soils where drainage is bad, there will be too much water retention in the topsoil. Digging it over will be of help and applying manure and compost will also help increase the worm population. Worms are nature's way of bringing air into the soil as they bore through and perforate the soil.

DIGGING IN MANURE.

FEEDING AND CONDITIONING THE SOIL

COMPOST

You can buy compost for improving the soil, but if you can make your own, it is free and it means you are truly recycling waste. Make your own compost by using vegetable and paper waste from the garden and kitchen.

Include the following:

- Vegetable waste such as carrot tops, lettuce leaves, vegetable peelings, pea pods.

- Kitchen waste such as tea bags, tea leaves, coffee grounds and crushed egg shells.

- Lawn mowings, plant waste, discarded foliage from shrubs.

- Chopped or shredded prunings from shrubs that are not too woody.

- Cardboard inner tubes, paper egg boxes, shredded newspaper.

- Straw and bedding from pets.

- Cut flowers that have finished.

FILLING A COMPOST BIN.

Don't include the following:

- Plastics, metals or foil.

- Any waste meat, fish or cooked foods, as these will attract rats.

- Perennial weeds and annual weeds that have lots of seed pods and particularly avoid bindweed or ground elder as these will not be killed off by the composting and could re-spread.

- Diseased plants – these should be destroyed by burning.

15

An enclosed compost heap works better than an open one as this will stay warmer and encourage decomposition. An open one may cool down and dry out before the matter has fully decomposed. In a well made heap, waste should compost within three months in warm weather and six in cold weather.

Making a compost heap

There are various composting bins available for sale, but it is easy to make your own from wooden planks. A small plot or garden needs a bin with capacity of about 0.5cu.m., but two heaps, side by side are ideal as one can be filling up while the second is decomposing.

Make sure the bin has a base open to the soil to allow worms to enter and speed up decomposition. Solid sides will keep in the heat generated by the process of decomposition. A lid or cover such as an old carpet, a large piece of wood or thick plastic sheeting, will hold in the heat and keep the rain out. Make sure it is easy to reach the contents so that you can turn the compost over with a fork to incorporate air, essential for the composting process.

LEFT: SPREAD VEGETABLE TRIMMINGS OUT IN AN EVEN LAYER.

RIGHT: ADD GRASS CLIPPINGS TO THE HEAP IN A THIN LAYER.

- Build up the heap with 20cm layers of vegetable waste.
- Wet straw can be layered between this. Spread farmyard manure or sulphate of ammonia over alternate layers or use a proprietary activator over each layer.
- Water the heap as you build it up and when it is full, cover it over with 2.5cm of soil.
- If the heap goes cold or dries out before it has finished decomposing, turn it over with a fork so that the top layer ends up in the middle, watering as you dig it over.

DIGGING IN MANURE.

FEEDING THE SOIL

The best way of feeding and enriching the soil is to add plenty of well-rotted farmyard manure and vegetable wastes that have been composted. Inorganic fertilisers with chemicals usually promise to give fast results, but they are usually washed out of the soil and may cause damage to the natural eco-system on your plot. Proprietary organic fertilisers can be used where necessary for a limited period such as:

- Seaweed fertiliser – either ground or liquid – make good soil conditioners as they encourage bacterial action.
- Fish, blood and bone meal, which contain a high percentage of nitrogen, encourage root growth.

- Hoof and horn fertiliser is handy when manure supplies are short as this slowly releases nitrogen into the plot.

Green manure

Green manure is a way of fertilising the soil by growing a crop and then digging this back into the soil to add nutrients. Growing a green manure crop during the winter is particularly useful as it helps to lock in nutrients that would be washed away by winter rains and snow. When dug into the soil in Spring, the foliage adds a good source of nitrogen and it is beneficial to practice green manuring as part of a four year crop rotation.

GREEN MANURE.

Some green crops have nodules on their roots containing bacteria which help fix in nitrogen and these crops need to be dug back into the soil while they are young and green.

Green manure crops include:
- Lucerne – Medicago sativa
- Broad Beans – Vica faba
- Red Clover – Trifolium pratense
- Mustard – Sinapsis alba
- Italian rye grass – Lolium multiflorum

Fertilisers

Some plants will need extra fertilisers to reach their peak.

Vegetables
- Peas, beans, onions, leeks, lettuce, celery and radish may be given lots of manure and compost for best results.

- Cabbages, Brussels sprouts, cauliflower, broccoli, kale and spinach should be given general fertilisers and lime, if this is indicated by a soil test.
- Beetroot, carrots, turnips, swedes, parsnips, celeriac and chicory need only a general fertiliser.

Fruit
- Soft fruit needs fish, blood, bone meal and garden compost.
- Fruit trees should be planted in deep soil with plenty of compost and if the soil is acid, add a little lime.
- Fruits with stones, such as cherries like plenty of lime, but fruits with pips such as apples, prefer less.

RAISING PLANTS NATURALLY

Seeds

- Always buy the best quality seeds to avoid disappointment.
- Store the seeds in a cool place until you can sow them, as heat or warmth can destroy the germinating properties of the seeds and they will fail to grow.
- In sheds or outside buildings, keep seeds in an airtight tin to prevent mice getting to them.
- If you collect your own seeds from plants, place these in envelopes and store in an airtight food container and keep in a cool place over the winter months.

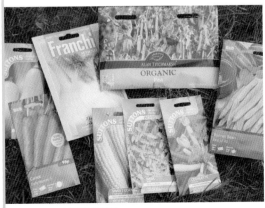

SELECTION OF SEEDS.

SOWING INDOORS

If you grow crops inside in trays, you can get ahead of the planting season and you will need to:

PREPARING SEED TRAYS.

- Fill trays, pots or biodegradable pots with fine multipurpose compost. Stand them in water until the compost is thoroughly wetted.
- Sow the seeds on top, thinly spacing by 1-2cm. An easy way to do this is to pick up the seeds individually on a wetted knife blade and position them one at a time.

PLANTING SEED TRAYS.

COVER LIGHTLY WITH DRY COMPOST.

- Lightly cover with dry compost or vermiculite, then level the surface gently.
- Cover with a sheet of glass, plastic or a polythene bag.
- Remove the cover every day to prevent damping off and check to see if the seeds have germinated.
- When first pairs of true leaves appear, bring the tray into full light.

Pricking out indoor seedlings

- Fill new pots or trays with John Innes No.1 potting compost and make holes in this deep enough to take the seedlings and roots.
- When the young seedlings are large enough to handle, loosen their roots with a small stick and prick them out – hold them by the leaf, not the stem. Replant the seedlings up to their necks.

- Using a fine rose on a watering can, gently water in the seedlings. Keep the trays out of direct sunlight for 2-3 days.

Hardening off

Plants grown in the greenhouse will need to be hardened off to acclimatise them to colder conditions, before planting outside. Otherwise, if they are taken from the warm indoor conditions to colder ones, the plants may not survive the shock.

- Put the plants in a cold frame outside and open the lid by degrees each day.
- If you do not have a cold frame, stand the plants outside in a sheltered spot for a few hours in the middle of the day.
- If the weather is still cold when the plants are hardened off, protect with plastic sheeting for a few days.

21

PLANTING OUT SEEDLINGS.

Planting out

Once the seedlings have hardened off, they are ready to transplant to your plot. You will need to:

- Water well before you transplant the seedlings.
- Prepare the ground and lightly dig it over. Use a string line to mark straight rows.
- With a trowel, make a hole deep enough to take the seedling. Plant the seedling up to the stem and settle in the soil.
- Using a fine rose, give the row a good watering.

OUTSIDE PLANTING

The best seeds for planting out of doors are those which germinate easily, hardy crops like peas and beans and those which dislike being transplanted.

Preparing a bed

- Dig over the bed and leave it to settle for a few days.
- Rake the ground previously dug over and stretch a string line down the rows.
- Make straight shallow drills in the soil using the end of a bamboo cane.
- Water the drill lightly then sow the seeds evenly and thinly – this will prevent the need to thin out later. Place the seeds in the palm of your hand and sprinkle them into the drill. Don't sprinkle directly from the packet or you will use too many seeds.

RAKING OVER A SEEDBED

THE ALLOTMENT GARDENER

PREPARING THE DRILL.

PLANTING SEEDS BY HAND.

- Cover the seeds and fill in the soil by shuffling along the rows and pushing the soil back over the drill.
- Write labels to give the name and sowing date of the crop.

Thinning seedlings

Thinning, or removing extra seedlings, is essential to give each plant enough good growing space to allow it to flourish and mature. Distances will vary with the crop, but thinning must be carried out before the plants become established and start to compete for space and light. When the seedlings have grown their first true leaves, pull up or pinch out the leaves of the weaker ones, leaving the strongest plants only. Pinching out is best for crops like carrots and onions as the soil is not disturbed by pulling up the roots, which may encourage carrot or onion fly to lay their eggs.

THINNING OUT PLANTS.

Transplanting

Make sure the seedlings are well established with at least four true leaves and a good root system. If planting seedlings grown in pots or modules, water well before planting out. Knock plants out of pots by tapping the rim to release the rootball. If plants have been grown in modular cells, carefully cut these away to avoid damaging the roots. Hold each plant by the leaves and make a hole deep enough for it to be planted just below the first leaves. Set the plant in the hole and firm it in gently around the roots. Water in and label the rows of plants. If planting on a hot day, keep the seedlings in the shade or in a plastic bag to help prevent them from drying out.

Weeding

- Perennial weeds with creeping root systems like ground elder or deep tap roots like dandelions, must be dug up and burned. Remove even the smallest pieces of root as these will re-grow.
- Annual weeds will gradually decrease over the years if you ensure they are not allowed to flower or seed and remove them as soon as you see them.
- Hoeing removes weeds before they grow and develop into larger plants.
- Mulching round plants will cut out light and stop emerging weeds from coming through, but this cannot be done until the vegetable seedlings are through.

TRANSPLANTING A SEEDLING.

WEEDING BETWEEN SEEDLINGS.

Watering

It is at a deeper level that roots need water. Check by pushing a finger into the ground. It can look very wet on the top, but be bone dry a short way under the surface. In dry weather it is better to water less often but thoroughly. This encourages deeper roots, which have a reserve to draw on. Light, frequent watering encourages roots to grow near the surface and these will suffer in dry weather.

Watering seedlings and plants

- After seedlings have just been planted out in rows, they can only take up a little water at a time so will need daily and light watering.
- Leafy vegetables will need a lot of water throughout their growth.

- Fruiting vegetables such as cucumbers and tomatoes benefit most if they are watered well when flowering and when the fruit starts to swell.
- Root vegetables will need little water in their early stages.

Mulching

Mulching means adding a layer of material on top of the soil to stop it from drying out. It also has a number of other benefits:

- Mulching can warm up the soil, depending on what material is used.
- Materials like black polythene or biodegradable paper will act as a weed control, because they cut out the light from growing weeds. The papers can be dug into the soil at the end of the season.
- Compost and manure mulches will be drawn into the soil eventually by worms and so will continue to feed the soil and improve the structure.

WATERING A ROW OF YOUNG PLANTS.

PESTS AND DISEASES

PROTECTING YOUR CROP

Cloches

Cloches will protect crops from frost, heavy rain and birds. They come in various forms, but glass or plastic are the two basic types.

- Glass cloches are good, but liable to breakage.
- Plastic sheeting is cheap and easy to store and can be easily assembled over a wire frame every year.
- Make sure the frame is wide and high enough to allow room for the plants to grow.
- Tunnel cloches are an excellent way of protecting rows of vegetables.

They are constructed of wire hoops and covered with plastic sheeting and can be used as one long tunnel or divided into shorter sections. The wire frames will need to be pinned or weighted to the ground to stop them blowing away.

Cloches for early vegetables

In colder climates you can start to grow many crops about a month earlier than usual if they are protected by cloches. These crops include early broad beans, cabbage, cauliflower, early peas, spinach, turnips and beetroot.

For these early crops, position the cloches in place about three weeks before they are required in order to let the soil warm up. Make sure the earth is wet when you position the cloches, as they will then help to conserve moisture from the ground.

Lifting the cloches by degrees will allow the plants to harden off gently. To start, open the ends during the day and then close them in again at night.

After protecting an early crop, the cloches can be used to cover young vegetables such as tomatoes, peppers and courgettes. In mid-summer another sowing of early vegetable crops can be made and the cloches used as mini greenhouses to mature the crops into early autumn.

Black polythene sheeting

If you want to start sowing early, particularly potatoes, tomatoes, peas and beans, use black plastic sheeting to help keep the ground warm, stop weeds growing and retain moisture. Firmly anchor the sheeting down over the surface of the prepared bed after sowing seeds. Once the seeds start to come up, make slits in the sheeting to let the plants grow through. Leave the sheeting in place until you harvest.

SHINY CDS WILL FRIGHTEN BIRDS AWAY.

Bird protection

Birds will love the tender new shoots of vegetable crops such as peas or lettuces. The following cost little and will help protect your crops:

- Tie old CD discs onto strings and thread them across two sticks to catch the sunlight and frighten away birds.

- Place empty plastic drink or transparent detergent bottles onto tall bamboo stakes. As they shake in the wind, they will rattle and make a noise to scare the birds.
- Pieces of thread tied to sticks in a zig-zag fashion will make an effective barrier against larger birds like pigeons.

Protecting fruit

- Protect less hardy fruit trees from frost when in blossom. Cover with fine netting.
- Currant bushes and gooseberries may need protection from frosts and when in flower, so cover the bushes with fine netting, which will also protect the fruits later on.

Wasps

Keep wasps away from fruit by placing a jam jar full of beer, covered with paper with a small hole cut in the top. As the wasps enter the jar they will be trapped.

Protecting Vegetables

Aphids

Aphids attack plants and suck out the sap, sometimes transmitting viruses at the same time. They breed very quickly so act as soon as you detect them to avoid infestation.

TOP: WASP FEEDING ON A PEACH.
LEFT: ENCOURAGE LADYBIRDS, AS THEY ARE FRIENDLY VISITORS.
RIGHT: SLUGS LOVE YOUNG SEEDLINGS.

- Slug traps sunk into the ground can be made from old plastic cartons filled with beer. The slugs are attracted by the smell, fall in and drown.
- Slugs will not crawl over sharp textures, so surround the seedlings with material such as eggshells or coarse, sharp grit.
- Place a wooden plank in the vegetable plot overnight and turn this over in the morning. The birds can then feed off the slugs and snails attached to it.

- Spray with a fine water spray or dab with a soft brush dipped in water with a dash of washing up liquid in it.
- Plant flowers in between vegetable rows such as pot marigolds or poppies, to attract the aphids onto them.

Slugs and snails

One slug can demolish a whole row of seedlings as they can eat twice their body weight in foliage, so they are particularly partial to delicate lettuce and cabbage seedlings. There are many measures to protect against slugs:

Flying pests

- Flying pests such as cabbage white butterfly, pea moths, carrot fly and cabbage root fly will attack vulnerable crops.

CABBAGE WHITE BUTTERFLY.

- The easiest way to protect against these is to erect a protective mesh cage over the crop that will allow light and rainwater in, but keep out the flying pests. Make a frame by stretching a fine mesh sheet over staked out short bamboo canes or wires.
- Protect brassicas from cabbage root fly by placing collars around the stem of each plant made from felt or old carpet underlay.
- Carrot root fly are attracted by the smell of carrots. Plant carrots in between onion rows to disguise the smell or thin out the seedlings to lessen the smell.

Gardeners' friends

An organic system in your plot of land, should let pests take care of themselves and encourage beneficial insects and animals to feed off the pests.

- Although birds may eat fruit and some tender shoots, they will also help protect crops by eating slugs, snails, caterpillars and aphids.
- Hedgehogs are wonderful garden predators. Encourage them with cat or dog food and provide them with a wooden hibernation area in winter, such as a box or log pile lined with some hay to keep them warm.
- Toads and frogs eat slugs and insects. A small pond or large plastic box sunk into the ground full of water, will attract frogs.

PROTECTIVE NETTING OVER CABBAGES.

HEDGEHOGS CAN BE A GARDENER'S BEST FRIEND.

Safer pesticides

As a last resort, you may have to resort to pesticides and fungicides to protect your crops. Organic pesticides only remain active for a day or two, so won't harm animals, but they should always be used with care. If you can, try to garden without using them. This is better, but if a fungus disease persists, an organic pesticide is the only answer.

Alternative and natural methods

- Marigolds, nasturtiums and poppies attract hover flies which eat aphids, so grow these next to crops such as broad beans.
- Grow rows of carrots in between onion rows to protect from carrot fly.

31

WEEDS

IDENTIFYING WEEDS

There are two types of weeds — annual weeds such as groundsel and chickweed, which grow from seed in one season, and perennial weeds such as dock, bindweed, couch grass and thistles, which will thrive for more than two growing seasons. One weed can scatter many thousands of seeds near and far, so it is important to remove all weeds before they flower and set seed, otherwise you will be weeding for many years to come.

Dealing with weeds

Weeds will only be able to grow if there is bare soil waiting for them to grow on, so it is vital to plant up, or cover bare patches on your plot. It is important to keep the immediate area around newly-planted plants and bushes, completely free of annual weeds as these will compete for the valuable nutrients and moisture in the soil that the plants need.

Regular hoeing just below the surface will help control persistent weeds. Slice the weeds off just below the soil, preferably when the soil is dry and keep the vegetable plot well hoed throughout the growing season.

Perennial weeds are more difficult to control because you will have to remove the entire root as well as the top growth. If you leave any scrap of root, the weed will grow back again. This can be hard work with weeds such as dandelions and thistles, which have a long taproot. These are best forked up, holding the stem close to its base as you pull up the whole weed.

LEFT: REGULAR HOEING WILL CONTROL WEEDS.
RIGHT: THISTLES ARE PERSISTENT WEEDS AND MUST BE DESTROYED.
TOP RIGHT: REMOVING THE WHOLE ROOT WILL PREVENT RE-GROWTH.

THE ALLOTMENT GARDENER

Weed killers

If you have a serious weed problem, using weed killer is the final option. There are two main types – contact weed killers, which kill only the parts of the weed they touch, and systemic weed killers, which will kill all parts of the weed.

Using weed killers safely

Follow the instructions on the pack and avoid using chemicals near fruit, vegetables and herbs. Perennial weeds can be removed with a spot treatment weedkiller.

PREPARING A NEW BED.

GROWING ORGANICALLY

Growing organically is not difficult and you can enhance the soil with organic additives instead of chemicals to supply the nutrients your plants need. The difference between natural and synthetic fertilisers is not always clear cut, as some products labelled as natural, are highly processed.

Natural fertilisers

'Organic' or 'natural organic' are the terms used to describe fertilisers that are as close to natural as possible. Check the labels on natural fertilisers. If the main ingredients are bone-meal, dried blood or other animal derivatives, the fertiliser is close to a natural state.

Natural fertilisers will feed plants more slowly than their chemical counterparts. Most natural fertilisers will help the soil retain water and nutrients and these are often in a slow release form. This helps produce even growth as the nutrients gradually become available to plants over time.

Organic fertiliser for a new bed

The best fertilisers for a new bed are composted and well rotted farmyard manure, well rotted garden compost or dried seaweed. Dig over the soil and break up any solid clods of earth. Dig in the compost to a depth of 15cm and fork over the material with the soil.

NATURAL FERTILISERS WILL ENRICH THE SOIL.

ROTATING YOUR CROPS

For success in vegetable gardening, you will need to practise crop rotation. Vegetables can be put into three groups, which match their different soil and mineral requirements:

Legumes
Peas and beans, plus sweet corn, spinach, chicory, endive, globe artichokes, onions, leeks, garlic and salads.

Brassicas
Cabbages, Brussels sprouts, broccoli, cauliflower, plus swede and turnip.

Root Vegetables
Carrots, parsnips, beetroot, salsify, celeriac, plus marrows, melons, cucumbers, aubergines, potatoes and tomatoes.

Crop rotation is vital for success in allotments or large scale vegetable plots. You will need to divide your plot into three and grow each of the above groups in its own area. Each year, move everything onto the next space, so that the same crops never grow in the same ground for more than one year in three. There is less risk of plants contracting root diseases and each year, the different crops will receive exactly the right type of soil preparation and will benefit from the nutrients the last crop has left in the ground.

> PLAN AS FOLLOWS:
> **Year one**
> ROOT VEGETABLES, BRASSSICAS, LEGUMES
>
> **Year two**
> LEGUMES, ROOT VEGETABLES, BRASSICAS
>
> **Year three**
> BRASSICAS, LEGUMES, ROOT VEGETABLES

EQUIPMENT

BASIC TOOLS

If you are just starting off, you may be tempted to buy a lot of equipment, but these are the basic essentials you will need.

A spade and fork – buy ones the right length for your height.

Stainless steel tools are expensive but will last a lifetime and soil will not stick so heavily to them.

A hoe – for weeding between rows of vegetables and marking out.

A trowel – for making holes and planting out seedlings.

A hand fork – for hand weeding.

String and garden canes for marking out lines and staking

KEEP TOOLS CLEAN AND DRY.

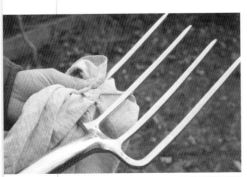

REGULAR CARE WILL PROLONG THE LIFE OF GARDEN TOOLS.

Storage and care

To keep all tools in good condition, store in a dry place such as a shed or garage as water will rust metal and destroy wooden parts. To keep metal parts in top condition, remove all soil after use and rub with an oily rag to keep your tools free from rust when spades and forks are in storage over the winter months.

WATERING

Rain water is free and is best for your plants, so you will need a method of collecting this. A water butt attached to a down pipe from a shed roof is ideal, but recycled large open containers such as clean industrial bins or an old sealed up bath tub can be used to good advantage.

You will need a good watering can – choose one with a good capacity and a fine rose for watering seed drills after sowing as these are too delicate to water in with a hose.

WATER USING A FINE ROSE — RAINWATER IS BEST FOR CROPS.

Vegetable Crops

Vegetables have always been an essential part of life and are vital for creating healthy meals that provide the vitamins and minerals needed for a balanced diet. The range of vegetables that can be grown at home is enormous, and whether you are skilled or just beginning, you will love raising plants from tiny seeds to maturity. The real pleasure of vegetable gardening lies in the freshness and flavour of crops just gathered from the plot, and watching the small investment you made on seeds turn into a regular supply of food for the table.

ASPARAGUS
- asparagus officinalis

- Perennial
- Height 1-1.25m
- Spread 0.5.-1.25m

Asparagus is the first treat of the season, so growing these delicious spears lets you indulge in a little luxury every spring. This vegetable is expensive to buy in the shops, but grow your own and you will find it very economical. Over the years, you may get 20 or more crops from the same bed.

VARIETIES

Martha Washington – these thick purple tinged green shoots have a long cutting season from May to June.

Conovers' Colossal – available as seed or crowns. Good for any soils. Freezes well.

PLANTING

Raising from seed
You can raise plants from seed but there will be a three-year delay between sowing and your first crop. Sow seeds outdoors in early April in drills 46cm apart. The seedlings can be transplanted the following year. A quicker way to establish an asparagus bed is to buy crowns.

Buying crowns

Buy healthy crowns with firm roots and avoid those with damaged roots. One-year-old crowns are best as they quickly establish a good root system. Keep crowns moist until you can plant.

Where to plant

Choose a bed in full sunlight if possible, and plant in rich well-drained soil. Moist, sandy soil rich in organic matter is best. A nearby hedge or fence is ideal to protect against wind.

Planting asparagus crowns

- Dig over to remove weeds and fork in 10cm of well-rotted manure or organic compost. Dig a trench 38cm wide and 25cm deep.
- Rake in a general purpose fertiliser and mound up 5cm of soil in the base of the trench. Spread the roots of the crowns over the mounded soil so that they spread out, spacing the crowns 46cm apart.
- Cover with 5cm of soil and water-in well. As the stems appear, fill in the trench so that the soil is 5cm above the ground.

AN ASPARAGUS BED

Special care

Eventual heavy cropping depends on slowly building up the crowns in the soil. Do not cut any spears until the third season after planting.

IN SEASON

Spring
Plant crowns and mulch.

Summer
From June onwards, allow the ferns to grow and build up reserves in the crown below the soil for the following year.

Autumn
In October, cut back the fern when it turns yellow. Apply a 5cm layer of manure or compost and mound up the soil over the row.

PICKING AND STORING

The season for cutting lasts from April to late June. Cut all spears when they are 15cm above the ground, regardless of their thickness.

Cut or snap the spears 5cm below the soil surface. It is important to cut the spears cleanly to encourage the plant to continue cropping.

PESTS AND DISEASES

Adult asparagus beetles and the larvae feed on shoots and foliage. Pick these off by hand or use an organic pesticide to control them.

RIGHT: SNAPPING OFF SPEARS FROM THE GROUND WITH FINGERS

AUBERGINE – Solanum melongena

- Annual
- Height 1m
- Spread 75cm

Aubergines are plants of tropical origin and can be grown under cover or outside in warmer southern regions in sheltered conditions. One or two plants can be grown in containers or growing bags in a protected corner and will yield good crops.

VARIETIES

Long Purple – produces good yield of dark purple fruits 15cm long.

Moneymaker – can be grown outside in warmer areas or in cold frames or cloches and is tolerant of lower temperatures. Good crops of tasty purple fruits.

Short Tom – small early cropping variety. Good for smaller plots or containers, cold frames or cloches in warmer areas.

PLANTING

Sowing seed

- Sow seed in early spring. For growing outside, sow ten weeks before the last frosts are expected. Sow in seed trays, pots or modules of moist seed compost. Sprinkle over 3mm compost then cover with glass and newspaper.

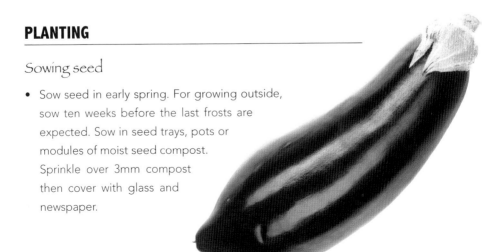

- When three leaves appear, prick out the seedlings into peat pots.

Harden off the plants gradually if planting without cover.

Where to plant

Only the sunniest and most sheltered sites produce good crops outdoors. Cloches and cold frames can provide the extra warmth and humidity needed in colder areas. Soil should be warm, well drained and moisture retaining.

Before planting, fork in a slow release fertiliser or dig in organic compost.

Planting the seedlings

- In April – May when the danger of frost is over, cover the soil with sheeting or cloches to warm it. Plant the seedlings in rows 24cm apart, spacing the plants 60cm apart. Erect a screen made with polythene sheeting round the plants to give extra protection, if possible.

- Pinch out the growing tips when the plants are 30cm high. Stake with canes or tie in the plants to wires for support.

DEVELOPING FRUITS NEED PLENTY OF SUN

Special care

- When the flowers start to open spray lightly with tepid water to help pollination.
- Feed the plants with a liquid fertiliser until well established, then feed with a high potash liquid fertiliser or tomato feed every ten days until the fruits form.
- Remove all but 5-6 developing fruits on each plant and pinch out any new flowers that form.

IN SEASON

Spring
Sow the seeds under glass.

Summer
When danger of frost is over, plant outdoors.

Summer/Autumn
Water sparingly but regularly. Feed regularly.

PICKING AND STORING

When the fruits are 20cm long, shiny and a rich purple colour, cut them close to the stem with a sharp knife. Do not let the fruits become over ripe or they will become bitter. Store for two weeks in a refrigerator.

PESTS AND DISEASES

Check for aphids and whitefly. If they occur, spray early with pyrethrum or insecticidal soap.

PLANTING IN GROWING BAGS GIVES GOOD RESULTS

BEETROOT
~ Beta vulgaris

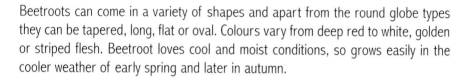

- Annual
- Height 15-20cm
- Spread 10-15cm

Beetroots can come in a variety of shapes and apart from the round globe types they can be tapered, long, flat or oval. Colours vary from deep red to white, golden or striped flesh. Beetroot loves cool and moist conditions, so grows easily in the cooler weather of early spring and later in autumn.

VARIETIES

Detroit 2 dark red – red globe type with a sweet flavour. Good for later planting and cropping.

Boltardy – deep red globe type, smooth skinned and a good cropper for early sowings.

Burpee's Golden – beautiful orange skin and yellow flesh. Best picked small and good flavour for salads.

PLANTING

Seeds

In most cases each corky seed is a cluster of 3 small seeds, so each planting will produce several seedlings which will need thinning out.

To improve germination, soak the seed first in a shallow dish of water

SOAKING BEETROOT SEEDS IN A BOWL OF WATER HELPS GERMINATION.

Where to plant

Choose a site in full sun if possible. Rich, well-drained light soil that has been dug in autumn and over-wintered is perfect.

Scatter on a slow release fertiliser 2-3 weeks before sowing.

If soil is heavy clay, plant in raised bed incorporating sand to lighten.

Planting beetroot seed

- Remove any weeds and dig the soil over to a depth of 30cm.
- Sow beetroot in rows 30cm apart. Sow seed about 3cm apart and 2cm deep.
- When the seeds germinate, thin out all but one seedling in each clump.

Special care

Don't over water the rows of seedlings or excessive leaf growth, with small dry roots can occur.

BEETROOT READY FOR HARVESTING

IN SEASON

Spring
Sow seeds as soon as the soil is warm and can be worked over.

Summer
Thin out seedlings and hoe between the rows to keep down weeds. Do not touch the roots with the hoe, or this will cause damage.

Autumn
Harvest and store the beetroot.

PICKING AND STORING

- Planting rows in small batches will give crops every two or three weeks.
- Pull the round varieties when they are large enough and have a diameter of about 4cm. Pull up by hand if possible, as lifting with a fork can pierce the flesh and cause bleeding during cooking. Twist off the leaves carefully leaving on about 5cm of stem and leave the roots intact.
- Place trimmed beetroot on their sides in a box of sand and store in a frost-free place up to the following March.

PESTS AND DISEASES

Beetroots are generally trouble free, but plants grown too closely together can attract the carrot fly, so thin out the seedlings to give plenty of space between them.

Rough patches on the surface are a sign of boron deficiency.

BROAD BEANS – Vicia faba

- Annual
- Height 0.3-1m
- Spread 50cm

Broad beans are the hardiest of the legume family. Crops planted in November can be enjoyed as the first beans harvested in spring, or plant early spring for harvesting later that summer. These beans are delicious served when small and tender, and if you have a glut, they freeze very well.

VARIETIES

Aquadulce Claudia – harvest from late May onwards. A long pod variety for autumn and spring sowings. Extremely hardy, less susceptible to black fly and good for freezing.

Express – harvest late May onwards. Fast maturing long pod with plump, green beans. Hardy with up to 30 pods per plant.

The Sutton – harvest May–August. Compact dwarf variety ideal for smaller plots. Bushy plant with large crop of good flavoured beans.

PLANTING

Where to plant

- Do not grow broad beans in the same plot for two years. Choose a sheltered sunny site with good drainage as they will rot in waterlogged soil.

Planting broad beans

- Choose winter hardy varieties for planting in November, or sow in early spring.
- Dig over the plot in autumn adding plenty of well-rotted manure or organic compost.
- Mark out rows 46cm apart and 7.5cm deep. Sow the seeds singly 20cm apart.
- Drive in stakes 90–120cm high for tying in the plants later.

Special care

- Hoe around the plants regularly, and when they are tall enough, tie in the plants to stakes with soft twine to support them.
- When the plants are in flower, pinch out the top 6cm of shoot to reduce the danger of black fly feeding on the young shoots, and to encourage development of pods.

BROAD BEAN PLANTS IN FLOWER

IN SEASON

Spring
Sow in mild areas.

Summer
Pinch out tops of spring grown plantings when in flower, and harvest winter grown crops.

Winter
Plant in November for next spring's crop

PICKING AND STORING

Pick when the beans begin to show and before the pods become too large. Snap downwards or cut the beans off with scissors to avoid uprooting the plant. Store in pods in the refrigerator, or shell and store in plastic bags in the refrigerator. To freeze, shell, blanch the beans in boiling water for 2 minutes; plunge in cold water and freeze. Keeps 12 months.

PESTS AND DISEASES

Mice and jays can steal some of the seeds just after planting. Blackfly or black bean aphid is the most common problem for broad beans. Control by pinching out the tops as soon as the young shoots and flowers appear.

BELOW: BROAD BEAN SEEDLINGS, RIGHT: PODS ON THE VINE READY FOR PICKING.

FRENCH BEAN – Phaseolus vulgaris

- Annual

There are a considerable variety of beans in this group, ranging from dwarf plants, which are ideal for smaller plots, to the climbing varieties, which will need space to grow and room for cane supports.

VARIETIES

Dwarf French beans
- Height 50cm
- Spread 20cm

The Prince – long slender pods with an excellent flavour. Crops well over a long period. Good for freezing.

Masterpiece – the most popular dwarf variety with long green crisp pods with a delicious flavour. Abundant crops.

Climbing varieties
- Height 2m
- Spread 30cm

Romano – an old variety, tender and tasty with a prolific crop. Ideal for freezing.

Blue coco – a purple podded variety that turns dark green on cooking. Delicately flavoured. Rapid growth and continues to crop for 10–20 weeks.

PLANTING

Where to plant
French beans dislike cold, wet soil, so for successful germination, delay planting until the soil is heated to 10°C. Don't grow in a shady site as French beans need full sun to flourish. Fertile, well-drained soil is best for strong growth and seeds may rot in heavy or clay soil.

Planting french beans

- Prepare the ground by digging a layer of farmyard manure in during the winter months. Broadcast and dig in a general fertiliser such as Growmore, two weeks before planting.
- Prepare the seed bed by raking level and making 5cm-deep drills 46cm apart for dwarf beans, and 60cm apart for climbing beans. Sow individual seeds 10cm apart. Rake soil over the drill and water well.
- Cover with a plastic cloche if sowing early in spring. When seedlings appear, hoe to keep down weeds. Mulch with straw or grass cuttings to retain moisture and keep down weeds.

Special care

Cold weather can turn the leaves yellow in early plants, so protect the young plants with horticultural fleece if a late frost threatens.

RAKING OVER A SEED BED BEFORE PLANTING.

IN SEASON

Spring

Sow from early May when the soil has reached 10°C. Make more monthly sowings until late June or July for crops all summer long.

Summer

Keep the bed moist but not wet until the seedlings appear. When the beans flower, water carefully, avoiding splashing the foliage.

Mulch to keep down weeds and retain moisture.

HOE CAREFULLY AROUND SMALL BEAN SEEDLINGS.

PICKING AND STORING

- Pick the pods when they are young and extra tender. They should snap in half with no signs of stringiness.
- Pick regularly to encourage more pods to form and so encourage bigger crops.
- Pick with scissors or hold the stems as you pull the beans away in an upward movement to avoid disturbing or uprooting the plant.

PESTS AND DISEASES

Halo blight is a bacterial seed-borne disease which will produce stunted yellow plants that soon die. It appears on leaves and pods as dark patches, and a characteristic yellow halo forms round the dark spots. Spraying with weak Bordeaux mixture can help control it, but if plants are badly affected, dig up and destroy them.

LEFT: HAND-PICK THE PODS FROM THE VINE.

RUNNER BEAN
– Phaseolus coccineus

- Annual

Runner beans follow French beans and are at their best during late summer and autumn. They come in dwarf varieties, which need no cane supports and can be harvested about 7–8 weeks after planting, or as tall, growing climbers, which take ten weeks or more to reach a harvest and will need cane supports.

VARIETIES

Dwarf Varieties
- Height 30-60cm
- Spread 15cm

Hammond's Dwarf Scarlet – ideal for a small plot. Early maturity with medium crop of tender sweet beans over ten weeks.

Pickwick – produces early crops of tender juicy beans. A prolific cropper. Beans need to be picked young.

Stick or Climbing Varieties
- Height 2.5m
- Spread 60cm

Kelvendon Marvel – tasty long stick beans. Matures early and crops heavily.

Scarlet Emperor – the most traditional variety with a heavy yield and tasty pods.

PLANTING

Where to plant

- Runner beans need full sun and warm weather. For rapid growth, the soil must be at least 13C for seed to germinate. Sow from early spring to late summer in well-drained soil in a sunny site.
- Careful preparation of the site and soil gives higher yields, so prepare a 60cm-wide trench a single spade's depth and fork in large quantities of well-rotted farmyard manure or garden compost into the base before replacing the soil.
- In April, rake in a general fertiliser. In colder areas use cloches to warm up the soil.

SOWING RUNNER BEAN SEED IN DOUBLE ROWS.

Planting and growing runner beans

- In early May sow the individual seeds 15cm apart in two drills spaced 60cm apart.
- Make a support for the beans by inserting bamboo canes into the soil 30cm deep. Space the canes 15-30cm apart, cross into a 'V' shape and fasten. Place horizontal canes in the centre for extra stability. For smaller areas, make a wigwam of crossed canes.
- Tie the young bean plants loosely to the cane supports and train 1–2 plants round each stake.

In June and July mulch around the established plants with straw or grass clippings.

Special care

Bushy growth can be encouraged in climbing beans by pinching out the tops of the main stems when they are around 25cm high.

TYING UP YOUNG BEANS TO THE CANES.

IN SEASON

Spring

In cooler areas sow seed indoors in pots of seed compost. Harden off and plant outdoors from late spring protected by cloches or fleece. Erect canes and plant out seeds after danger of frost has passed.

Summer

Harvest beans when young and pick continuously to encourage production of more pods.

Autumn

Leave some pods to ripen on the plant at the end of the season. Dry them and store in an airtight jar in a cool place for next season.

At the end of the crop, cut down the visible parts of the plants and dig in the roots to provide a valuable source of nitrogen.

PICKING AND STORING

Pick when the pods are young and tender. The pods are in prime condition for harvesting when they snap cleanly when bent. Store in a cool place for 2–3 days or slice, blanch in boiling water, cool in cold water and freeze in plastic bags.

PESTS AND DISEASES

Grey mould and halo blight can cause damage in wet and humid weather. If plants are badly affected dig up and destroy them.

Slug damage and black bean aphid may be annoying, so try to pick these off as you detect them.

RUNNER BEANS ON THE VINE

THE ALLOTMENT GARDENER

BROCCOLI
~ Brassica oleracea

- Annual
- Height 40-75cm
- Spread 30-75cm

Broccoli, sprouting broccoli and calabrese are healthy green vegetables and, as well as bursting with taste and flavour, this vegetable group is a marvellous source of vitamin C, folic acid and iron. For year-round supplies, sprouting broccoli is grown as a winter crop for picking in spring and calabrese can be picked from summer into autumn.

VARIETIES

Sprouting
Purple Sprouting Early – easy to grow, prolific and hardy with abundant side shoots. Ready for cropping late winter to early spring.

Purple Sprouting Late – similar to the early varieties with good tasty heads. Ready for cropping mid to late spring.

Calabrese
Express Corona – plant first for cropping early in late summer. Good large compact heads.

Green Comet – plant early for cropping in early autumn. Large dark green flower heads and plenty of side shoots.

Romanesco – plant last for cropping late autumn. Produces heads over a long period. Lime-green heads are delicate and delicious steamed.

PLANTING

Growing indoors

- For early spring, crops, grow indoors in trays from late summer to autumn. Sow in modules or seed trays in moist potting compost.
- Harden off and transplant seedlings from late winter to early spring. Transplant when they have two pairs of true leaves and are 7–8cm high.

SOWING SEEDS.

Where to plant

Choose a plot that is well drained and has not grown a brassica crop recently. Broccoli thrives on a plot which has been well manured and has recently produced early potatoes. To reduce the risk of club root, add lime to the soil in autumn or a top dressing in spring.

WATERING.

Planting broccoli seedlings

- Water the seedlings the day before transplanting. Handle carefully and plant the seedlings at 46cm intervals. Water in well.
- Heap up soil around the stems as they grow to anchor them and prevent rocking in the wind. With larger varieties, stake to support against the wind.

ABOVE & BELOW: TRANSPLANTING.

Special care

- When the central heads have formed, cut these before the flowers open. The plant will grow more heads on the side shoots and regular harvesting encourages formation and growth.

IN SEASON

Spring
Sow seeds in trays two months before the last frosts of spring. Harden off seedlings.

Summer
Plant out seedlings. Keep well watered. Feed with a general-purpose liquid fertiliser. Check for pollen beetles and mealy aphids.

Autumn/Winter
Heap up soil around the plants for extra support if they are top-heavy. Protect with netting against pigeons.

PICKING AND STORING

Cut the florets or stems when they are 15–20cm long. Cutting encourages new side shoot formation and each plant should have a 6–8 week harvest. Do not completely strip the plant or allow it to flower, as this will stop growth. Store florets in a plastic bag in the refrigerator for 2–3 days or blanch and freeze soon after picking.

PESTS AND DISEASES

- Dip the roots in an anti-fungal solution to protect against cabbage root fly. Cabbage caterpillars feed on flower heads and do most damage in dry summers, so pick these off. Watch for aphids and whitefly and look for the eggs on the underside of the leaves.

BRUSSELS SPROUTS
- Brassica oleracea

- Annual
- Height 1m
- Spread 40-50cm

There are many varieties of Brussels sprout. These can be mainly divided into the old-fashioned varieties which produce tall plants with heavy yields of large sprouts. The new F1 hybrid has even, compact growth and stems tightly packed with small uniform button sprouts.

VARIETIES

Peer Gynt – F1 hybrid – compact plant good for smaller plots. Medium-sized sprouts packed tightly onto stems with high yield.

Winter Harvest – conventional variety with good all-round performance. Good flavour and keeping qualities. Later cropping with high yield.

Rampart – good flavour and stores well. Late cropping and good disease resistance.

PLANTING

Sowing in the seed bed

- Prepare a seed bed or frame in an open, sunny but sheltered site. Before sowing, rake in a general-purpose fertiliser such as Growmore. If cabbage root fly is a problem, rake in Bromophos before planting.

In early spring, sow seeds in shallow drills about 2cm deep in rows spaced 15cm apart.

Where to plant

Brussels sprouts need a site in open sun. Deeply dug soil, rich and prepared with compost, will produce best results, but do not dig this in just before planting.

Planting in a permanent bed

- Prepare the previous autumn, if possible, digging in well-rotted garden compost. The ground should not be freshly manured as this will cause excess nitrogen and the sprouts will 'blow'. Double-dig over the plot.
- Transplant the seedlings into rows 90cm apart with 75cm between plants. Plant firmly with the lowest leaf at soil level.
- After planting, tread soil around the roots so that the plants will not blow over. Hoe regularly and water young plants in dry weather.

EARTHING UP SOIL AROUND THE BASE OF THE PLANTS.

Special care

- Earth up the soil at the base of each plant to encourage root formation and keep stable in winds. Stake to keep upright in winds if necessary.

IN SEASON

Spring
Sow outdoors in seedbeds, keep well weeded.

Summer
Transplant seedlings. Water well and earth up.

Autumn
Stake tall varieties and harvest early crops.

Winter
Sow early varieties indoors in trays. Harvest late crops.

PICKING AND STORING

- Harvest when the sprouts at the base are walnut-sized and tightly closed. Gather sprouts from the bottom upwards, snapping off with a downward movement, or cutting off with a knife. In cold weather, whole plants can be lifted and stored in a shed for several weeks.

HARVEST THE SPROUTS ON THE STEMS OR PICK A WHOLE STEM.

PESTS AND DISEASES

- Club root can be a problem with Brussels sprouts. Remove all diseased plants and destroy them. The best way to prevent this is to rotate crops, making sure that no brassicas were grown in the plot the year before.
- Powdery mildew is a white deposit that can cause young plants to yellow and die. This can be a problem when the roots are dry. Water and mulch and spray leaves with a fungicide. Leave plenty of space in between plants, helps prevent mildew spreading.

CABBAGE – Brassica oleracea

- Biennial grown as annual for cutting
- Height 30-75cm
- Spread 30-50cm

Cabbage is indispensable for the vegetable plot and it is extremely hardy and easy to grow. As the many different varieties mature at different times it is possible to have cabbages for cutting almost all year round. Choose the types to grow each season for delicious, crisp, tasty leaves, rich in beta carotene and vitamin C.

VARIETIES

Spring Varieties

Offenham Compacta – early spring cabbage with dark green leaves.

Greensleeves – spring greens variety with good textured leaves. Early cropping.

Pixie – small, tight and compact hearts. Good for small plots as can be closely spaced. Crops very early.

Summer Varieties

Derby Day -ball headed cabbage for harvesting early summer.

Hispi – pointed heads with excellent flavour. Good for small plots and close spacing.

Ruby Ball – red cabbage with a solid uniform shape. Good flavour for salads. Crops until January.

Late Summer Varieties

Stonehead – tightly packed and early maturing crop.

SAVOY CABBAGE

Wivoy – savoy type that resists frosts with good compact green head. Crop until late April.

Winter

January King 3 – drumheaded Savoy type, extremely hardy and frost resistant. Crops mid autumn to early winter.

Christmas Drumhead – tasty type with puckered green leaves.

PLANTING

Growing in trays

Sow seeds indoors in modules or trays to be ready for planting about five weeks after sowing.

Growing in seedbeds

To make a nursery site, dig over firm soil and rake in a general-purpose fertiliser. Make seed drills 15cm apart and 1cm deep. Sow the seed thinly and cover with a fine tilth. Water in; when the seedlings are 10cm high transplant carefully.

Where to plant

Choose a site open to full sun. If the soil is acidic, add lime. Make sure that you follow a three-year crop rotation and do not grow brassicas in the same place each year. Well-drained soil rich in organic matter will produce the best crops.

Planting cabbage seedlings

- Water the seedlings well before transplanting. Using a dibber, make holes at 30cm intervals in the prepared ground. Space the rows 30cm apart. Place in the holes and loosely return the soil.
- About two weeks after planting, heap up a little soil around each seedling to protect against frost lifting the plant; firm in the plants.
- Sprinkle a little dried blood around each plant in March to encourage large heads. Water regularly in dry spells and hoe regularly between rows to keep them weed-free.

SAVOY CABBAGES IN ROWS.

Special care

Providing plants are healthy, you can produce a second crop after cutting. After cutting off the head, cut a cross in the stump 1cm deep, from which should sprout a new growing cluster of smaller cabbages.

IN SEASON

BABY CABBAGE

Spring

Plant seeds in trays or in a cold frame. Harden off before planting out in March or April.

Spring/Summer

Transplant seedlings in April/May. Feed with a fertiliser.

Summer/Winter

Sow spring cabbage seedlings. Water and hoe regularly.

PICKING AND STORING

Pick tender spring cabbage and as needed as these do not store well. Cut the heads before they become too large.

Winter types can be stored for longer. Red cabbage or tightly packed heads can be stored after harvesting and will keep for 1–2 months if stored on slatted shelving in a frost-free shed.

PESTS AND DISEASES

- The cabbage white caterpillar will eat the leaves and heart. Spray this yellow, black spotted pest when first seen or protect the cabbages with micromesh netting.
- Plants that wilt in summer and then recover quickly may have club root, a fungus that swells roots. Plants with club root must be destroyed immediately. Protect against this by growing your own seedlings and dipping these in a solution of thiophanate methyl. Don't buy in seedlings as these may carry the fungus.

THE ALLOTMENT GARDENER

CARROTS – Daucus carota

- Annual
- Height 15-30cm
- Spread 15cm

The flavour of tasty young carrots freshly pulled from the soil, is hard to beat. Most of us are familiar with the bright orange varieties of carrot we all love, but they also come in purple, yellow and white varieties. There are several groups of carrot which harvest throughout the year, so with successive sowings, you can have plenty of fresh crops maturing at different times.

VARIETIES

Short-Rooted
Amsterdam Forcing 3 – short, slender rooted and tasty. Good for freezing. Crops very early.
Navarre – sweet and tasty with a good rich colour. Crops heavily.

Intermediate
Autumn King – broad, stump-rooted and well coloured. Robust and hardy, good resistance to carrot fly. Crop – maincrop or late.
Nantes Tip Top – tasty, sweet and well coloured. Cylindrical uniform roots with no hard cores. Maincrop.

Long-Rooted
St.Valery – long, evenly tapered roots, good for exhibiting. Maincrop.
New Red Intermediate – very long tapered roots that store well. Maincrop.

PLANTING

Preparing a seed bed

- In winter, dig the soil over well and deeply. For heavy or clay soils, mix in a layer of sand or grit to lighten the soil. Apply a general fertiliser.
- From March onwards, rake the soil over into a fine tilth and make drills 1cm deep and 15cm apart. Sow the seed thinly, then lightly cover the drills with soil.
- Thin the seedlings regularly after the first 5cm-high leaves appear. Water and firm back the rows after thinning.
- Hoe between the rows regularly. Pull the early sowings from mid-June onwards when they have dark foliage.

Where to plant

All carrot crops thrive in light, open textured soil that is fertile and free-draining. Heavy clay soils or soils which have been freshly and heavily manured, are not suitable for carrots. Sandy or loamy soil free of large clods or stones is best. Choose an open site in full sun.

Planting the seeds

- As carrot seed is very fine, mix the seed with some fine sand to make even sowing in neat rows easy. Sowing the rows closely together, makes for less maintenance in the vegetable plot.

IN SEASON

Spring

Sow early varieties. Warm ground under cloches for earlier harvests. Wait until March or April for sowing in open beds.

Spring/Summer

Sow maincrop varieties in open beds in April and May.

Autumn

Lift and store maincrops before frosts begin.

THINNING OUT A ROW OF CARROTS

AVOID DAMAGE — LIFT CARROTS WITH A FORK.

PICKING AND STORING

- You can lift carrots at any time, but they are at their best when small, tender and sweet.
- Lift the maincrop for storing. Gently and carefully ease up the carrots with a fork to avoid damaging them.
- To store in winter, remove soil from the carrots and cut off the leaves about 1cm above the crown. Place between layers of dry peat or sand in a wooden box, making sure they do not touch. Store in a cool place or shed until March.

PESTS AND DISEASES

Carrot fly can be troublesome as the flies lay their eggs in the soil, then the yellow larvae will tunnel into the carrots causing considerable damage and making them inedible. Sowing rows of carrots and onions alternately, can help as the strong smell of the onion leaves deters the fly. A 1m-high barrier of polythene around the carrots can help keep the fly away.

CAULIFLOWER
~ Brassica oleracea

- Annual
- Height 50-65cm
- Spread 50cm

Cauliflowers are a little more difficult to grow and need more attention than other brassicas but the taste of tender home grown cauliflower is really worth the effort. Cauliflowers are a good source of vitamin C and other vitamins. If you want to grow for the freezer, choose varieties with smaller heads as these have firmer young florets that freeze well.

VARIETIES

Summer Varieties

Dominant – good for dry conditions, and produces firm white curds with leaves that curl over for protection. Good for freezing. Harvest midsummer.

Early Snowball – dwarf and compact, good for smaller plots. Reliable variety and heads will not discolour in bad weather. Good for early harvests from June.

Autumn Varieties

White Rock – a versatile variety with a pure white curd. Vigorous growing and self-blanching. Harvest from July to October.

All the Year Round – forms large milk-white curds protected by large green leaves. A reliable variety that will mature throughout the year depending on the date of planting.

Winter Varieties

'Walcheren Winter 3-Armardo April' – solid pure white curds are hardy and frost resistant. Good flavour for eating raw in salads. Crops April onwards.

Veitch's Self Protecting – the hardiest variety of all, with large incurved leaves that give protection to the milk white curds. Crops until January.

PLANTING

Sowing seed indoors

- Ten weeks before the last frost date, sow seeds indoors in pots of moistened compost. Sow two seeds per pot. The plants are ready for transplanting when they have 5-6 leaves. Harden the plants off gradually.

Where to plant

Cauliflowers thrive in full sun and moderate weather. Avoid frost hollows. Deep, rich, fertile well-drained soil is needed for successful cultivation. An alkaline soil that has not recently grown another brassica, is essential for good crops. If the soil is not alkaline, it must be well limed and rich in humus and plant food. Strawy manure or organic garden compost should be dug in as preparation.

SEEDLINGS IN DIVIDED TRAYS

Planting cauliflower seedlings

- Three weeks before the last frosts, work compost into the ground to be planted and dig over the ground deeply.
- Make sure the ground is warmed to at least 10C. If it is too cold, the heads or 'curds' will not form.
- Water the seedlings in the pots. Lift them carefully and plant at 60cm intervals in rows 60cm apart. Water in the transplanted seedlings and check that they are firmly planted. Apply a suitable insecticide to the soil around the plants to combat cabbage root fly.
- Hoe to keep the weeds down and earth up the stems to prevent the plants from shifting in the wind.

Special care

To protect the developing curd from sun and rain and to keep it white, break a leaf over it, and secure.

IN SEASON

Spring

Sow seeds indoors ten weeks before the last frost. Harden off the seedlings gradually, before transplanting.

Spring/Summer

Plant out seedlings and keep well watered and mulched. Plant a succession of seeds of different varieties for a harvest that will last up to November.

Summer/Autumn

Apply a liquid feed regularly and water well. Harvest the crops.

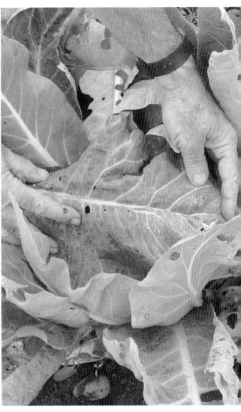

COVERING THE CURDS WITH A LARGE CAULIFLOWER LEAF HELPS KEEP THE CENTRE WH

PICKING AND STORING

To harvest cauliflowers, squeeze them before cutting, to see if the heads are firm. Cut the heads in the morning and harvest when the curds are tight, before they separate and become seedy.

PESTS AND DISEASES

Watch out for aphids, whitefly, flea beetles and caterpillars. To protect against club root, dip the roots of the seedlings in trichlorphon to deter the cabbage root fly.

CELERY – Apium graveolens var.dulce

- Annual
- Height 30-60cm
- Spread 20-30cm

There are two basic types of celery, – trench and self-blanching. Trench is so called because of the method used, where soil must be heaped up around the stems to exclude sunlight and blanch the stems. Harvested from late spring, this type is very hardy and has a strong, delicious flavour. More recently, self-blanching varieties have been developed. These have a shorter cropping season, from mid-summer-to mid-autumn. They have a less intense flavour and smaller stems, but are easier for amateur gardeners to grow successfully.

VARIETIES

Trench

Giant Pink – huge crisp pale pink stalks that blanch easily. Harvest from mid-late winter.

Giant White – an old tall variety, with crisp white stems and a solid heart. Good flavour for salads. Harvest until February.

Hopkins Fenlander – late-maturing green stems of medium size with a good string-free texture. Harvest mid-late winter

Self-blanching

Golden Self-blanching – has a compact white yellow heart and sturdy, self-folding stalks. It has a delicate flavour with a crisp, string free texture. Harvest late autumn onwards.

Greensleeves – attractive pale green sticks with a tasty flavour. Harvest late autumn onwards.

Celebrity – crisp, well-flavoured, heavy stalks. Bolt resistant and good for early cropping in autumn.

PLANTING

Planting celery seed in trays

Sow seed from mid- to late-spring in trays of moistened seed compost. Scatter the seed thinly over the surface, but do not cover with compost. Spray lightly with water. Keep the tray in a propagator or a greenhouse at 13°C. Germination may take several weeks. Repot when the seedlings have two pairs of true leaves, then gradually harden off the plants before planting out.

Where to plant

- Celery requires cool conditions and flourishes at 15-20°C in an open site. It needs fertile, moist, yet well-drained soil that is slightly acid. Add lime to acid soils before planting.
- Rotate crops and do not grow celery where brassicas have been grown in the previous year.

Preparing for planting

- In March or April, dig trenches 30m deep and 40cm wide, about 90cm apart. Fork over the trench base and work in well-rotted manure or compost. Return the soil to a level of within 7.5cm of ground level. Leave the trench open until early summer.

Planting self-blanching celery

Plant out the seedlings in May in a square, not a row, 27cm apart or 15cm apart for a higher yield of smaller heads.

Planting trench celery

- Plant in well prepared soil in late May or June. Plant the seedlings at 23cm intervals in staggered double rows 23cm apart.

- When the plants are 30cm high, loosely tie the stalks just below the leaves or wrap paper collars or corrugated cardboard around the leaves and tie securely.
- As the plants grow, earth up the soil about every three weeks into a mound around the plant, leaving plenty of leaf above the soil and being careful not to let soil fall into the hearts. Earth up only when the soil is damp.

Special care
- Feed the plants with a liquid fertiliser about every three weeks.

IN SEASON

Early Spring
Sow seed indoors, ten weeks before the last frosts are expected.

WRAPPING PAPER COLLARS AROUND THE STALKS AND MOUNDING UP SOIL ROUND THEM.

Spring/Summer
Harden off the plants and transplant into the soil. Hand weed around the plants as celery produces so many roots near the surface; a hoe can damage these.

Winter
Cover the trench with straw in cold weather to protect from frosts.

PICKING AND STORING

Begin harvesting the heads when the outer stalks are large. Lift the heads carefully with a trowel, or if the roots are long, use a fork. Cut away the stalks and wash well before use.

PESTS AND DISEASES

Watch out for carrot and celery fly larvae. These eggs on the foliage in summer months attack leaves and make them blister and decay. The blisters may be pinched out, but to prevent an attack, spray the foliage during June and July with quassi solution which will prevent the flies from laying their eggs.

CELERIAC
– Apium graveolens
var. rapaceum

- Annual
- Height 50cm
- Spread 30cm

Celeriac is a delicious root vegetable and is a type of common celery, also know as turnip-rooted celery. This is an easy winter vegetable to grow as it is hardy and more disease-resistant than celery. The bulbous root has a tangy celery flavour and is delicious raw in salads, or made into piping hot soups.

VARIETIES

Alabaster – a high-yielding and vigorous variety with round bulbs and good resistance to bolting. Crops from August–December.

Iram – medium-sized bulb shape with few side shoots. Remains white when cooked. Stores well. Harvest until January.

Marble Ball – reliable globe variety, good cropper and strongly flavoured. Stores well. Harvest until January.

PLANTING

Planting in seed trays

- Celeriac has a long growing season and the young plants are sensitive to cold, so success depends on strong seedlings. Sow in late spring in a propagator at 18°C or in late spring in a greenhouse, or under cloches.

SCATTERING CELERIAC SEED IN A COMPOST-FILLED SEED TRAY.

- Plant seeds in seed trays or modules in a peat substitute compost. Germination may take a little time and growth will be slow. When the seedlings are large enough to handle and about 1cm tall, pot them on.
- Harden off the seedlings when the weather is warmer in late spring.

Where to plant

Choose an open site in direct sunlight where the soil is rich and retains moisture. Heavy, moist soil gives good results. A week before planting, apply a general purpose fertiliser.

Planting celeriac seedlings

- Plant in late May, after the seedlings have hardened off. Plant in rows 38cm apart and at 30cm intervals. Do not bury the crowns, but plant at ground level. Water in thoroughly.
- Water well in summer and apply a mulch of compost around the plant to keep in moisture. Water in a liquid feed in summer.
- The roots will be ready for lifting from September but in mild areas they can be left in the ground until the following spring. Protect the crop in the ground against frost damage with a covering of straw or bracken.

CELERIAC PLANTS IN THE SOIL.

Special care

Remove the outer leaves in late summer to expose the crown. Remove side shoots as they appear to encourage the bulb to develop.

IN SEASON

Spring
Sow seed inside in February-March or in a cloche or cold frame from April.

Summer
Harden off the seedlings and plant out in late May. Water regularly.

Autumn
Remove side shoots from the crown.

PICKING AND STORING

Ideally, leave the bulbs in the ground until they are needed. Harvest in the winter when the bulbs are about 12cm diameter. Lift carefully with a fork, trim away the roots and leaves and store in boxes of sand or sawdust in a dry, frost-free shed. Store in the refrigerator for up to a week.

PESTS AND DISEASES

Celery fly can be a pest and in spring the larvae tunnel into the leaves, causing blisters. Pick off any brown blistered leaves. Growing under fleece can protect the young plants.

CHINESE CABBAGE
– Brassica pekinensis

- Annual
- Height 35cm
- Spread 25cm

A quick-growing oriental vegetable, this brassica has dense heads with a mild flavour. The crisp pale green leaves have thick white veins and are ideal for salads or cooking. There are three main types of this vegetable: the compact barrel shape with a dense heart, tall cylindrical shapes and long, loose-leafed varieties.

VARIETIES

Barrel varieties
Kasumi – easy to grow barrel type with a round compact head that will resist bolting. Harvest 55 days after sowing.

Eskimo – self-blanching variety with a large sized head. Green outer leaves with a pale white centre. Quick-growing – harvest 45 days after sowing.

Tall varieties
Jade Pagoda – tall cylindrical hybrid with a firm crisp head. Good resistance to cold weather. Harvest 70 days after sowing.

Ruffles – delicious flavour with pale green open leaves. Semi-hearting and early maturing 55 days after sowing.

Loose leaf varieties

Santo serrated leaf – Good resistance to cold and suited to northern climates. Open, loose serrated leaves. Harvest 50-70 days after sowing.

Tah Tsai – a non-hearting cabbage. The leaves can be cut regularly as a 'cut and come again' vegetable. Harvest 45-60 days after sowing.

PLANTING

Preparing the seed bed

Dig over the soil deeply before planting. If the soil is acidic, dig in lime. Remove any large stones and break up clods of earth. Rake over to a fine tilth.

Where to plant

Choose an open sunny site with deep, moisture-retaining but free draining soil with plenty of organic matter incorporated. An alkaline soil is ideal, or add lime to acidic soils. Ideally, grow after a crop of potatoes.

Planting Chinese cabbage seed

- Make 2cm deep seed drills spaced 35cm apart. Sow the seeds at 30cm intervals in the drills then lightly rake the fine soil over to just cover them. Water in well.
- Water the rows regularly and start thinning out the seedlings when they are large enough to handle.
- Water regularly, as sporadic watering can cause damage to the heads. Feed with a liquid or granular general fertiliser. In late summer, tie up the leaves of the hearting varieties with raffia.

Special care

In hot weather keep the plants mulched and well watered, otherwise they may bolt.

IN SEASON

Summer

Sow from July onwards in situ, as the seedlings will not transplant well.

Autumn

Harvest after 45 days or longer.

PICKING AND STORING

Cut leaves from the loose-leafed tall varieties, as needed or cut away the whole heads of the barrel types. Cut the heads above the soil when they feel solid. Store in a frost-free shed for up to two months.

PESTS AND DISEASES

Flea beetles can make holes in the seedlings and leaves. Place a stickily greased plank of wood near the plants to attract the pests.

CHILLIES – Capsicum annuum

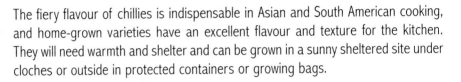

- Annual
- Height 60m
- Spread 40cm

The fiery flavour of chillies is indispensable in Asian and South American cooking, and home-grown varieties have an excellent flavour and texture for the kitchen. They will need warmth and shelter and can be grown in a sunny sheltered site under cloches or outside in protected containers or growing bags.

VARIETIES

Apache – red round fruits of good compact size.

Hungarian Yellow Wax Hot – good for growing in cooler areas. Long pointed fruits ripen to bright red.

Jalapeno – extremely hot tapering green fruits that ripen to red. Longer cropping period.

Habanero – small orange fruits with very hot fiery flavour.

PLANTING

Propagating chilli seeds

- Sow indoors in late spring in trays of modules of moist seed compost. Cover thinly with compost then cover with glass and newspaper.
- When three true leaves appear transplant into 6cm peat pots.

CHILLIES GROWING ON THE VINES.

Where to plant

For outdoor growing, a sunny sheltered site is vital; otherwise grow under glass, cloches or clear plastic sheeting. Light fertile, moisture-retaining soil will give best results.

Planting chilli seedlings

- Harden off young plants and plant outside under cloches or transplant into 23cm pots of compost or growing bags. Protect with plastic sheeting, cloches or glass.
- Provide cane supports for the plants as they grow.

IN SEASON

Spring

Sow under cover. Transplant the seedlings when danger of frost is over.

Summer

Keep weed free and water regularly. Harvest regularly to encourage longer cropping.

PICKING AND STORING

Pick the first fruits when they are green and glossy. Pick regularly to encourage further cropping. Fruits can be picked green and allowed to ripen into yellow orange or red. The heat of chillies will increase with the maturity of the fruit. At the end of the season, lift the whole plants and hang upside down in a shed to ripen the remaining fruits. Fresh chillies will keep for up to three weeks in the refrigerator. Chillies can be dried, pickled or frozen successfully.

PESTS AND DISEASES

Be aware of slugs, which can damage the foliage. Botrytis can rot fruits in cool or wet weather. Remove any decaying leaves or fruit immediately.

COURGETTE
~ Cucurbita pepo

- Annual
- Height 90cm
- Spread 90cm

Courgettes are marrows that are specially bred to be ready to pick small, delicate and sweet. As well as the green varieties there are colourful yellow types that really brighten up the vegetable patch. Most courgettes are bush varieties, but if growing space is restricted, try a variety suitable for training up a wooden trellis support.

VARIETIES

Ambassador – a high-yielding dark green fruit that crops heavily over a long period. Harvest until September.

Supremo – very tasty dark green speckled fruit. Compact in growth, so good for smaller sites. Harvest until September.

Golden Zucchini – golden-yellow fruit that needs to be picked young, or can mature into a marrow. Harvest until September.

DeNice Fruit Rond – a round fruit with a delicious flavour. Needs to be picked young. Harvest until September.

COURGETTE IN FLOWER

PLANTING

Planting in pots

From mid to late spring, fill pots with John Innes sowing compost. Sow two-three seeds in a 7.5cm pot, pushing the seeds 2cm down into the compost. In May, when the plants have formed their second pairs of leaves, harden outside gradually or in a cold frame.

Preparing a bed

- Dig the ground deeply and well. Rake over the surface and remove any stones or large clods of earth.
- Dig deep planting holes 60cm apart, with a width of 90cm between rows to allow for spreading. Fill each hole with well-rotted manure or garden compost and replace the soil to make a mound over each hole.
- In May, water the seedling well and carefully transplant them in the mounds, being careful not to disturb the roots.
- Alternately, plant two seeds directly into each mound in May and thin out when necessary.

Where to plant

Courgettes should be planted in full sun. An open site will have better air circulation and prevent attacks of mildew.

Special care

Warm the soil two to three weeks before planting out the seedlings, by laying down horticultural fleece over the prepared plot.

ALLOW PLENTY OF SPACE FOR EACH PLANT TO SPREAD.

IN SEASON

Spring

Sow the seeds indoors from the end of March. Harden off the seedlings gradually during late April or May.

Spring/Summer

Plant out when all danger of frost is over, in early to mid- May, or protect under cloches if there is still a threat of cold weather. Pinch out the growing points on the lateral branches when they are 60cm long and train them around the plant. Harvest when the courgettes are about 15cm long.

PICKING AND STORING

Check the plants regularly and pick the crop to keep the plants producing and putting this energy into new fruits. Cut the courgettes away with a knife about 2cm above the courgette.

PESTS AND DISEASES

Mildew appears as a white powder on the underside of leaves. If this is left, the foliage will turn brown and fall off. In humid weather spray with Bordeaux mixture to prevent an outbreak.

HARVESTING COURGETTES — CUT THEM AWAY FROM THE PLANT WITH A SHARP KNIFE.

CUCUMBER

– Cucumis sativus

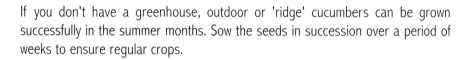

- Annual
- Height 1-3m
- Spread 1m

If you don't have a greenhouse, outdoor or 'ridge' cucumbers can be grown successfully in the summer months. Sow the seeds in succession over a period of weeks to ensure regular crops.

SHORT CUCUMBER

ROUND CUCUMBER

VARIETIES

Outdoor ridge varieties:

Burpless Tasty Green – trailing vine variety, with smooth skin. Tender, crisp and tasty, resistant to mildew.

Long Green Improved – robust, high yielding and reliable with long tasty fruits.

Masterpiece – a trailing vine variety with long, good flavoured fruits. Very productive and reliable plants.

Pickling varieties or gherkins:

Venlo Pickling – small gherkins with knobbly skins, ideal for pickling.

National Pickling – an old short, blunt variety with smooth fruits. Vigorous in growth and heavy yielding, ideal for pickling.

Gherkin – is very fast growing and produces masses of prickly fruits for pickling.

PLANTING

Preparing the ground

In early May, dig holes 30cm wide, spaced in rows 90cm apart. Dig to a depth of 23cm and fill them with organic compost or manure. Replace the soil so that it forms a mound.

Where to plant

Ridge cucumbers need rich, fertile, well dug soil in a sunny, but sheltered position.

Planting cucumber seed

- Sow three seeds in each mound, pushing the seeds down 2cm into the soil. Cover each planting with a halved transparent plastic bottle or large jar to encourage germination.
- When the seedlings produce the first pairs of true leaves, thin out to leave the strongest plant in each mound.
- Erect wooden trellis or netting suspended between canes to support plants and the fruits.
- Once the plants have produced 5-6 leaves, pinch out the growing points of the stems, allowing 2 laterals to grow evenly around the main stem. Train cucumbers and gherkins around the netting or tie in with soft twine.
- Keep all plants well watered. Feed regularly with a high potash fertiliser. Ridge cucumbers will be pollinated by insects

Special care

Outdoor varieties need less attention than greenhouse varieties. Keep plants well watered and apply a mulch over the roots to prevent misshapen fruit forming from lack of water as the young fruits begin to set.

ABOVE: PINCHING OUT SIDE SHOOTS.
RIGHT: GROWING ON A TRELLIS WILL SUPPORT THE VINES AND FRUITS.

THE ALLOTMENT GARDENER

IN SEASON

Spring

Prepare the ground and sow outdoors in May.

Summer

After the plants have set fruit, pinch out the side shoots so that the plant will put all its energy into growing fruits. Pinch out the tops of the vines before the first frosts of autumn; any last fruits set will then mature.

PICKING AND STORING

Ridge cucumbers and gherkins are best picked before any yellowing begins. Allow them to develop fully and do not pick fruits young, as they can be bitter. For bigger yields, pick fruit regularly, which will encourage heavier cropping.

PESTS AND DISEASES

Cucumber mosaic virus is a common problem that can cause poorly formed fruits. Remove all diseased parts or whole plants. Spraying with soft soap can help save a crop.

FLORENCE FENNEL
- Foeniculum vulgarae
var. dulce

- Annual
- Height 50-60m
- Spread 45m

This bulb-shaped vegetable has an attractive light feathery foliage which makes it an extremely ornamental vegetable. Fennel has crisp, overlapping layers with the texture of crunchy celery and a strong, attractive aniseed flavour. The bulbs can be sliced and eaten raw in salads or cooked as a delicious hot vegetable. The leaves and stalks can also be used in salads. There are two main types of bulbs – squat and elongated varieties.

VARIETIES

Cantino – squat variety, resistant to bolting. Good flavour and can be sown early so will be ready to harvest from late summer.

Fino – vigorous squat variety, with good resistance to bolting. Sow early for harvesting in August.

Perfection – long French variety with a delicate flavour. Sow in May for October harvesting.

Sirio – long Italian variety with compact sweet flavoured white bulbs. Fast maturing; sow in July to harvest in October.

PLANTING

Planting seed

From April to July, sow successive batches of seed thinly in individual modules. As soon as they can be handled, thin out the seedlings in the modules. Modules are preferable to growing in pots or trays of compost as this causes less root disturbance, which can lead to bolting. The seedlings will be ready for planting out when they have two true leaves.

Where to plant

Fennel grows well in a well-drained sheltered site. The soil must be warm and sudden changes of temperature or cold winds can cause the plants to bolt. So, some shelter or cloches may be needed in colder areas. Good fertile soil with organic matter dug in is vital for success.

PLANTING SEEDS IN PEAT MODULES.

Planting fennel seedlings

- Prepare the seed bed in the autumn, digging in plenty of organic compost. Four weeks before planting out, rake in a slow release general fertiliser.
- Space the seedlings at 30cm intervals in rows 46cm apart. Water well and firm in.
- Hand-weed between the plants or mulch with compost to keep down weeds and retain moisture. Water regularly.

Special care

Draw soil around the small bulbs when they are the size of a golf ball and continue to earth them up as they begin to swell. This will blanch the bulbs and can also be done by tying cardboard collars around the bases of the plants.

IN SEASON

Spring

Sow in peat modules in successive batches. Harden off the seedlings and plant out when they are small. Protect with cloches or fleece if cold threatens.

Summer

Hand-weed round plants and keep them well watered. Sow new plants.

PICKING AND STORING

Harvesting can begin when the bulbs have swollen. Cut beneath the bulbs just above ground level with a sharp knife, as the stem can re-grow tasty shoots. The bulbs should be eaten on the day of picking for maximum flavour.

PESTS AND DISEASES

Bolting or flowering, and producing seed prematurely, can be problems if the plants' growth is disturbed by cold or windy weather. Choosing bolt-resistant varieties and protecting with cloches will help. Don't leave the seedlings in pots to grow too large, or they will run to seed when transplanted.

SWOLLEN BULBS IN THE SOIL, WITH FEATHERY LEAVES.

GARLIC - Allium sativum

- Annual
- Height 60cm
- Spread 15cm

Garlic is easy to grow and is surprisingly hardy. You will find many varieties available, all adapted to particular climates and areas. Garlic is often grown from healthy bulbs saved from a previous crop, but if you are starting from scratch, buy nematode and virus-free stock. As garlic is used sparingly in cooking, you should be able to grow enough to keep you well supplied all year round if you tie and hang the bunches and store them in a cool, dry place.

VARIETIES

Long Keeper – is good for colder areas. White skinned, good-sized firm bulbs that keep well.

Solent Wight – heavy cropper with a mild flavour. Produces large white bulbs with lots of cloves on each bulb.

Elephant Garlic – sweet and mild in flavour. The larger sized bulbs will grow up to 10cm in diameter.

Rocambole – also know as 'Serpent Garlic' because of the coiled stem. Produces small red bulbs with a stronger flavour.

Germidor – an early cropper that produces large purple bulbs with up to 15 cloves per bulb.

PLANTING

Preparing the soil

Dig the plot over well. Ideally, grow on a plot well manured from a previous crop. If the soil is poor, rake in a general fertiliser 10 days before planting.

Where to plant

Garlic needs an open sunny site with well-drained soil. If the soil is heavy clay, grow in ridges or work in sand or grit into the topsoil to lighten the texture. Alkaline soil gives best results.

Planting garlic bulbs

- Garlic is best planted in late autumn, but can be planted in February. Break the bulbs into cloves and plant with the flat base downwards and the pointed ends upwards in rows at a depth of 2.5cm. Do not press the cloves down into the soil as this inhibits root development. Space them 10cm apart and leave 20cm between the rows.
- Hand-weed around the growing plants and keep well watered in early summer.

PLANTING OUT GARLIC CLOVES

Special care

- In late summer, when the leaves begin to yellow, gently loosen the bulbs from the soil and lift them with a fork.
- Lay the bulbs on the soil and leave to dry out in the sun. Handle as little as possible, as bruising at this stage can cause rotting in storage.
- If the weather is wet, dry the bulbs on trays in a shed.
- Don't leave the crop in the ground after the leaves have yellowed, as the crop will shrivel or become diseased during storage.

IN SEASON

Autumn

As garlic requires a cold dormant period of one to two months when temperatures are 0–10° degrees, it is better planted in late autumn to yield large bulbs. Plant cloves on a sunny site and mark the rows at each end in case the site gets covered in leaves.

Summer

Keep the plants well watered. Lift the bulbs when the leaves have turned yellow. Don't leave them in the ground for more than two weeks or the papery covering will deteriorate and the cloves will not store well.

PICKING AND STORING

When the bulbs and stems are dry, tie into bunches, or plait the stems together, or hang in open string bags. Hang in a cool dry place such as a shed or garage.

PESTS AND DISEASES

Garlic is hardy, but onion fly may lay their eggs around the bases and tunnel into the bulbs and the plant will yellow and die. Destroy any diseased plants. Rotating crops regularly can help prevent this.

JERUSALEM ARTICHOKE
– Helianthus tuberosus

- Annual
- Height 4-5m
- Spread 30cm

Jerusalem artichokes are also known as root artichokes. They are a versatile winter vegetable with a sweet, smoky flavour and come in creamy white thin-skinned slim varieties and purple skinned knobbly tubers.

VARIETIES

Fuseau – large long white tubers with smooth skins. Compact growth up to 2.5m.

Dwarf Sunray – the smallest variety of white tubers reaching only 2m in height. Thin-skinned tubers are crisp and tender and there is no need to peel.

Garnet – purple skinned variety with a good flavour. Tall growing.

PLANTING

Buying tubers
Buy named varieties of tubers from garden centres or choose firm tubers from the greengrocer or supermarket. Avoid dried-up tubers and choose smooth-skinned egg-sized or smaller sized and less knobbly ones for planting.

Where to plant

Choose an open position in full sun. Jerusalem artichokes will produce large crops in fertile, well-drained soil, but fair crops of smaller tubers in poor soils. Artichokes are good for breaking up heavy soils and will also provide a good windbreak or screen, as they will grow tall and bushy. In relation to other plants, however, remember that the row will take light from neighbouring low-growing vegetables.

Planting the tubers

- In February, dig over the planting area and make holes 15cm deep at 30cm intervals. Space the rows 90cm apart.
- Place an egg-sized tuber in each hole and cover with soil. Heap up a slight ridge of soil over each row and water in well.

Special care

- When the plants have reached 30cm height, earth up the soil around the base of each plant to help stabilise them.
- Stake the plants for support with canes or tie into wires.
- In midsummer, remove the flower heads and cut back the stems to 2m so that the plant's energy is concentrated in the tubers.
- In autumn, when the leaves begin to yellow, cut back the stems to 8cm above ground level. Leave the tubers in the ground to protect against frost and lift as needed.

PLANTING THE TUBERS.

A JERUSALEM ARTICHOKE PLANT AFTER TWO MONTHS' GROWTH.

IN SEASON

Spring
Plant tubers in February-March.

Summer
Keep weed-free, water and stake to support the plants. Remove the flower heads.

Autumn
Cut back the stems and begin harvesting

Winter
Store tubers for planting next year.

PICKING AND STORING

The tubers begin to soften after lifting, so leave them in the ground until needed. Add a covering of straw or the cut down stems to protect against frost. Use a day or two after lifting, or store in the fridge for up to one week. Take care to dig up all the tubers or they will regrow again during the next year.

PESTS AND DISEASES

Slugs or wireworms may hollow out the tubers and cause damage, but this is a relatively problem-free crop.

THIS TALL BUSHY ARTICHOKE PLANT CAN PROVIDE A WINDBREAK.

KALE – Brassica oleracea

- Annual
- Height 1m
- Spread 30-45cm

The dark green crinkly leaves of kale are a rich source of vitamin C and iron. Kale is one of the hardiest of winter vegetables and the leaves are best eaten young and tender and harvested regularly for a longer cropping season.

VARIETIES

Fribor – dense, curled, dark green leaves with good flavour. Hardy with good resistance to frost. Crops from late August.

Pentland Brig – is a cross between curly and plain leafed kale. Excellent flavoured young leaves and shoots and immature flower heads can be cooked like broccoli.

Thousand Head – plain-leaved tall variety and very hardy. Good for cropping from winter into spring.

Dwarf Green Curled – compact and hardy, good for smaller plots growing to 45cm height. Bushy dense leaves have a good flavour and are suitable for freezing.

PLANTING

Sowing

- In April or May, prepare a seed bed, removing any large stones and raking over well.
  Form 2cm deep seed drills spaced 15cm apart and sow the seed thinly along each drill. Lightly rake the soil back over and tamp down with the rake head. Water in.
- In late June to early August transplant the seedlings when they are 12cm high. Plant in rows 46cm apart with the lowest leaves just above the surface of the soil.
- In autumn earth up each plant around the base as a protection against frost and wind rock.

Where to plant

Choose an open sunny position. Kale will thrive in most soils, but add lime if the soil is particularly acid. Taller varieties may need staking in windy areas.

IN SEASON

Spring
Sow in drills on prepared ground.

Summer
Transplant the seedlings into beds and weed regularly. Water in dry weather.

Autumn/Winter
Pick leaves regularly to extend the cropping season. Remove any yellowing leaves in winter.

HOEING ROUND KALE PLANTS.

WATERING KALE PLANTS

PICKING AND STORING

Remove the young leaves when they are 10cm long with a knife. Cut leaves from several plants at one time. Harvesting regularly for constant young growth and a long cropping season. Young leaves and shoots are tender and delicious but the old ones may be tough and bitter.

PESTS AND DISEASES

Kale is the most tolerant of the brassicas to cabbage root fly and club root. Whitefly can be a problem if it infests the edible parts, so harvest the leaves regularly.

HARVESTING THE YOUNG LEAVES.

THE ALLOTMENT GARDENER

KOHLRABI
– Brassica oleracea Gongylodes Group

- Annual
- Height 70cm
- Spread 50-60 cm

This tasty brassica, sometimes known as stem cabbage, has an unusual ball-shaped swollen stem and ruffled green leaves. The ball is the main edible part and is eaten like a turnip, or shredded for salads, and has a crisp, mild, nutty taste.

VARIETIES

Purple Vienna – purple-skinned with mild flavoured white flesh. Ideal for later sowing and winter harvesting.

Green Vienna – pale green skin with white flesh. Early maturing variety.

Rowel – green-skinned with white flesh. Juicy sweet white flesh with a crisp texture.

PLANTING

Sowing seed indoors
In February-March, fill modules or pots with compost and press three seeds into each pot and water well. Keep in a warm position. Thin out the seedlings and harden off outside gradually, covering at night. Transplant in rows 30cm apart after the last frosts are over.

KOHLRABI READY FOR CUTTING.

Sowing in drills

From early April to September, mark out drills 2cm deep and 30cm apart. Sow three seeds together at 15cm intervals. When the first leaves appear, thin out the seedlings leaving one strong seedling 15cm apart.

Where to plant

Plant in rich, well-drained soil. Rake in a general fertiliser, or dig in organic compost before planting. Although the purple varieties will tolerate frost, a site open to full sun will produce best results.

Special care

Keep well watered and harvest when the bulbs are the size of a tennis ball. Do not allow the bulbs to grow too big, or they will become woody.

IN SEASON

Spring

Sow indoors in February to March, or outdoors in early April.

Summer

Thin out seedlings and water during dry periods. Feed with a high nitrogen fertiliser. Crop early sowings eight weeks after sowing.

Winter

Leave hardy varieties in the ground and harvest when needed.

PICKING AND STORING

Pull up the plants when they are the size of a tennis ball. Lift and store in boxes of sand or sawdust. Remove the outer leaves, but leave the central tuft in place to keep the bulbs fresh.

PESTS AND DISEASES

Cabbage root fly can cause stunted growth in the plants. Cut out discs of cardboard, or carpet underlay and slit halfway. Position a 'collar' around the stem of each seedling to prevent adults from laying eggs near the roots.

LEEK - Allium porrum

- Biennial, grown as annual
- Height 1m
- Spread 20cm

Leeks have a long growing season and these delicious sweet, onion flavoured vegetables can be harvested in the winter months. They are hardy and the white parts can be blanched by mounding up earth around them as they grow to produce a longer white stalk with a mild flavour and texture. The flavour of homegrown leeks is unsurpassed when compared to shop bought ones and they are a good source of potassium and iron, with smaller amounts of vitamin C and carotene in the green leaves. Leeks can be divided into two groups, long thin types and short stout types. As there are early, mid-season and late varieties, you can harvest right through winter.

VARIETIES

Early

Clarendon White – produces large sticks in autumn from a February sowing. Dark green foliage with long stems, with a sweet, mild flavour.

King Richard – long variety with a high yield. Hearty long stems with a good texture and mild flavour.

Mid-season

Cobra – medium length variety with good resistance to bolting. Good flavour.

Musselburgh – very hardy popular variety with long stems and an excellent flavour.

Late Season

Yates' Empire – thick stems that can be left in the ground until April. Broad green blades with pure white bases and sturdy stems.

Autumn Mammoth 2 – medium-sized straight thick stems, high yielding. Matures in late autumn and can be harvested until mid-spring.

PLANTING

Planting indoors

During late winter, or about 12 weeks before the last frosts, sow in modules, peat pots or seed trays of compost. When the seedlings are 5cm tall they are ready for transplanting.

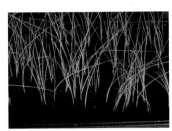

A TRAY OF HEALTHY LEEK SEEDLINGS.

Planting in a seed bed

• In late March to mid April, prepare a seedbed by digging over well and raking to a fine tilth. Sow the seeds thinly in 1cm deep drills, 15cm apart. In early May thin out the seedlings to 2.5cm apart.

PLANTING OUT THE SEEDLINGS.

Where to plant

Choose a plot open to full sun. Good drainage is necessary, as leeks will not thrive in heavy soils that remain wet in winter. Newly manured ground is not desirable and leeks are best planted in ground which has been manured for a previous crop. The ground should be dug over well during the winter, and any large clods or stones removed as the soil needs to be fine enough to earth up the leeks to help the blanching process.

Planting and growing

• Dig over the planting rows well and make 15cm deep holes with a dibber in rows 30cm apart. Drop one plant into each hole but do not fill with soil, fill with water.
• Weed and water the plants regularly and mound up soil around them to help blanching.

Special care

Longer white stems are obtained when the plants are earthed up. Gradually draw up the soil around the plants as they grow. Cardboard or tile collars can be placed around the plants to prevent soil getting into the plant centre. Continue earthing up until November when the tops of the leeks only will show above the soil.

IN SEASON

Spring

Sow seed in pots or in seed beds. Harden off seedlings and plant out after the last spring frost. If you can't plant your own seed, buy seedlings in pots, avoiding over large or wilted ones.

Summer

Mound up soil around the plants, weed and water.

Autumn/Winter

Begin harvesting as soon as the plants are large enough.

MOUNDING UP SOIL ROUND THE YOUNG PLANTS.

PICKING AND STORING

Leave the leeks in the ground and lift as needed. Lift with a fork to avoid damage, or pull up singly by hand using a trowel to loosen the roots. Store in a cold frame or cold shed for up to two weeks after lifting.

PESTS AND DISEASES

Rust may appear as orange spots on the outer leaves during wet summers. Remove infected debris and feed with a high potash fertiliser – foliage which develops later in the season may be healthy. If rust occurs, do not grow leeks on the same plot for the next four years.

MARROW - Curcubita spp.

- Annual
- Height 30-85cm
- Spread up to 3m

Marrows are easy to grow and these traditional fruits can be stored for use in the winter. You can choose to let the fruits swell and mature, grow one or two large fruits per plant, or grow six to eight small ones and eat these young and tender.

VARIETIES

Long Green Trailing – long-fruited variety, dark green with pale stripes. Prolific cropper in late autumn and stores well.

Tiger Cross – bush type, resistant to cucumber mosaic virus. Crops early and produces well.

Tender and True – semi-trailing type that matures early and can be cut as a courgette when young. Good resistance to cucumber mosaic virus.

Minipak – bush type with small striped green fruits. Fast growing with high yields.

PLANTING

Planting in mounds
- Make planting holes 1.5m apart a spade's width and depth. Fill the hole with organic compost or well-rotted manure. Replace the soil to form a raised mound, then water well.

- Soak the marrow seeds overnight and sow 2–3 seeds 2cm deep in each mound. When the seedlings have three true leaves, thin out to leave one plant in each mound.

Where to plant

Choose an open unshaded position in full sun, with good air circulation.

Rich fertile soil will produce the best results. Dig in organic matter before planting. For smaller plots with limited space, grow bush marrows.

Planting pot grown seedlings

- Sow seed in peat pots of compost indoors or in greenhouses in mid to late spring. From mid-May onwards, transplant in the peat pots, when the danger of frosts is past. Plant in mounds as above, and mulch around each mound.

Special care

- From mid-May onwards keep well watered. Water underneath the leaves, not over the plant. When the fruits begin to swell, feed with a liquid fertiliser.
- In June, pinch out the tips of the main shoots of trailing varieties when they are 60cm long and train them evenly around each plant.
- Hand pollinate if the weather is cold early in the season. Remove a male pollen, releasing flower and dust into a newly opened female flower, or paint on to the female with a fine paintbrush.
- Place straw under the developing fruits to discourage slugs.

YELLOW MARROW FLOWER READY FOR POLLINATING.

IN SEASON

Spring
Sow seed indoors in April in peat pots. In May, sow seed outdoors, or transplant pot-grown plants.

Summer
Water and feed well. Mulch with straw to conserve water.

Autumn
Lift fruits onto straw, wood, or bricks to discourage slugs and prevent rotting.

PLACE STRAW UNDER MARROW TO DETER SLUGS.

STORE MARROW IN A NET BAG.

PICKING AND STORING

When they have reached full size, gently push your thumbnail into the stalk. If it goes in easily, the marrow is ready for cutting. Cut the fruit away from the plant, do not pull the fruit away or the roots will come up from the soil. Harvest regularly and store the marrows in a cool place, or hang from a shed ceiling in a net bag.

PESTS AND DISEASES

Cucumber mosaic virus causes yellow mottled and puckered leaves, which will prevent growth and rot the fruit. Dig up the plants and burn them. Wash all tools and your hands afterwards.

ONIONS - Allium cepa

- Annual
- Height 30-60cm
- Spread 10-20cm

Onions can be divided into several groups according to their colour, shape and size. The common bulb shape can have brown, yellow, or red outer skin and is planted in spring to harvest in late summer. Japanese hybrid onions can be planted to overwinter, ready to harvest in spring or early summer. Shallots are smaller, with a concentrated flavour much prized by cooks and come in elongated or flattened bulbs with papery brown or pink skins. Button or pickling varieties are mini-onions, lifted small. Spring or bunching onions are picked small, complete with leaves for salads.

VARIETIES

Bulb

Ailsa Craig – straw-coloured large, round, well-shaped bulbs with a mild flavour.

Stuttgart Giant – white, flattened bulbs with a mild flavour. Good for keeping and slow to bolt.

Red Barron – medium-sized bulbs with a shiny crimson skin. Strong-flavoured red-ringed flesh, good for storing.

115

Shallots

Pikant – reddish-brown, medium-sized bulbs, with firm flesh and a good strong flavour. Stores well and resistant to bolting.

Hative de Niort – deep brown bulbs with an elongated spindle shape, white flesh and an intense flavour.

Pickling

Paris Silverskin – marble-shaped with very tight silver skins, good for cocktail onions.

Shakespeare – small brown onions, tasty and perfect for pickling.

Salad

White Lisbon – Very hardy, fast growing variety with thin skins. Produces tasty continuous crops over a long period.

Winter White Bunching – Slim stalks and mild tasting long leaves. Hardy and overwinters well.

PLANTING OUT SHALLOT SETS

PLANTING

Onion sets

Although onion sets are more expensive than seed, they have several advantages. They are quick to mature and so are a good choice for colder regions where the growing season is shorter. They will not be attacked by onion fly and will grow well in poorer soil.

Plant sets in shallow drills, push into the ground with the tips just above the surface. Space 5cm apart in rows 25cm apart. If birds pull up the sets, replant them immediately.

Where to plant

Onions need an open site with non-acidic soil with a pH of more than 6.5. and good drainage. The ground needs to be reasonably fertile, but not freshly manured. Do not grow onions on the same site every year.

Spring-sown onions

- In February to March, prepare a bed, removing all stones and weeds and rake in a general-purpose fertiliser 10 days before planting.
- In late February to March, mark out drills 30cm apart and 1cm deep. Sow seed thinly. In cold areas, sow seed under glass in January and plant out seedlings in April.
- Thin out or plant seedlings 5cm-7.5cm apart.

IN SEASON

Winter/Spring

Grow seeds inside in trays eight weeks before intended planting date.

Mid-Spring

Plant out seedlings and sets. Thin out seedlings grown from seed.

Summer

Lift, dry and store onions and shallots.

PICKING AND STORING

Bulb onions

Harvest when the weather is dry. Allow the bulbs and leaves to dry out while still in the ground and when the top foliage has bent over and dried out, lift carefully with

ROWS OF SPRING ONIONS.

a fork to avoid bruising them. Spread out in the sun to dry on sacking in late summer. Before storing, remove any damaged, soft or spotted onions and use these for cooking. Store in trays or net bags, or tie in ropes and hang from the ceiling in a cool place.

Shallots

Lift shallots in clumps when the leaves have turned yellow and dry. Divide the bulbs from the clump, remove loose soil from around the roots and rub away the loose leaves. Spread out to dry in full sun, turning the bulbs over occasionally. Store in slatted trays, net bags or old tights.

Salad onions

Lift these before the bases swell. Water well before lifting to make pulling easier. Use fresh as required.

PESTS AND DISEASES

Onion neck rot is a fungal disease that affects onions in storage and these must be destroyed. Dusting seed in fungicide when planting, helps prevent this.

Onion fly is a problem in dry soils. Covering with fleece helps keep the flies out until the crop has germinated.

ONIONS HANGING TO DRY.

ORIENTAL GREENS & LEAVES

MUSTARD LEAF

VARIETIES

Mizuna and mustard greens – *Brassica rapa & Brassica rapa var. nipposinica*

There are many forms of the leafy mustard greens range and these vary in flavour from mild to very hot. These are types of a Japanese brassica with glossy green foliage and stems that can be eaten raw in salads or cooked as spinach. Seeds can be obtained by post from specialist seed catalogues.

Mizuna has rosettes of attractive green leaves with juicy white stems with a mild flavour. The small plants will yield several harvests and are slow to bolt. Pick the leaves when young and eat raw in salads or cook in stir-fries or braises.

Mustard greens or Indian mustard has tender green leaves can be sown in June to September for an autumn harvest. Good for salads or stir-fries.

Komatsuna – *Brassica rapa var. perviridis*

Also known as mustard spinach, these round dark green leaves are mild, sweet and slightly spicy in flavour. The plants have a good tolerance to heat and cold. Eat them raw in winter salads, or cook as spinach. They can be harvested as small tender leaves or allowed to grow into large robust plants.

Pak choi – *Brassica rapa var. chinensis*

Also know as white celery mustard, this small plant has paddle-shaped leaves with a white central rib. Sow from June to August for a late summer crop.

PLANTING

Where to plant

Chose an open site with partial shade to keep summer crops shaded and cool. Soil enriched with well rotted manure will produce best results and faster growth.

Planting

- Sow seed in drills 1cm deep, spaced 15cm apart. When seedlings have two true leaves, thin them out. Use the thinnings for soups and salads.
- Water well and protect late autumn sown plants with plastic or cloches if leaving over winter.

PICKING AND STORING

Pick the leaves small and tender as soon as they are ready, which will encourage a regrowth. Use on the day of picking, as they will begin to wilt.

PESTS AND DISEASES

Flea beetles or cabbage root fly can be destructive. Growing under mesh or horticultural fleece can help protect the crop. Hand pick pests off, or brush lightly with soapy water to remove them.

PAK CHOI

PARSNIP – Pastinaca sativa

- Annual
- Height 15-35cm
- Spread 10-15cm

Parsnips come in three basic shapes and sizes: short and bulbous; intermediate longer or 'bayonet' shapes, with rounded shoulders and longer roots; and narrow, long-rooted types. In shallow soils, the shorter varieties are best, but the longer rooted types will thrive in well conditioned good deep soil. Parsnips are one of the oldest root vegetables and they make delicious soups, purées or accompaniments to roast meats.

VARIETIES

Avonresister – short, small bulbous roots with good sweet flavour. Good canker resistance and suits poorer soils.

White Gem – wedge-shaped, intermediate length. Excellent flavour with good canker resistance. Good for heavier soils.

Tender and True – long variety, tasty and sweet with little core. Good canker resistance.

PLANTING

Preparing a bed

- In December, double dig the soil over at least 30cm deep. If the soil below is solid, break this up with a fork.
- In February-March, remove any large stones or clods and rake in a general fertiliser 10 days before planting.

Sowing seed

- Make 2cm deep drills. As parsnip seed is very light and can blow away, sow on a still, windless day. Sow in groups of three–four seeds, spaced at 15cm intervals, in rows spaced 30cm apart.
- Lightly rake the soil over the seed and water in. Cover with horticultural fleece if possible, and remove when the seedlings come through.
- Start to thin the seedlings when the first sets of true leaves appear, leaving one strong plant at 15cm intervals.

PLANTING PARSNIP SEEDS IN 2CM-DEEP DRILLS.

Where to plant

Choose an open, sunny site, with a good depth of soil that can be dug to a depth of at least 60cm. Choose a spot that has not been recently manured. Well-drained, neutral, or slightly acid soil is best.

IN SEASON

Spring

Sow seed in late February to March, but avoid cold weather, as the seedlings will emerge in two to four weeks. To avoid poor germination, sow later when temperatures are over 7°C.

Spring/Summer

Thin out seedlings, and weed carefully between plants, taking care not to damage the crop. Water in dry weather.

Autumn/Winter

For best flavour, leave the crop in the ground until needed. Start lifting when the foliage begins to die down.

PICKING AND STORING

Although they will be ready for lifting from late summer, parsnips have a better flavour when they have been exposed to frost or low temperatures, around freezing point. Lift them with a fork to avoid damage. To store, remove the leaves and store in a cool shed, layered in boxes of sand or peat substitute, making sure they do not touch each other.

THINNING OUT PARSNIPS.

PESTS AND DISEASES

- Parsnip canker develops in the crown of the plants and causes the root to rot. There is no control but early sowing, lime-deficient soils, or aggressive hoeing, can damage the roots and encourage this.
- Carrot fly larvae can tunnel into parsnips. Growing under fleece cover can help limit this.

PEAS & MANGE TOUT

~ Pisum sativum

- Annual
- Height 0.6-2m
- Spread 30-60cm

Sweet garden peas and edible pea pods, such as sugar snap, or mange-tout, are a delicious treat in early summer. Peas are usually described according to the timing of the crop, early, second early and main crop, so choose the right variety for the planting time.

VARIETIES

Kelvendon Wonder – heavy cropping early dwarf pea, weather- and mildew-resistant. Small sweet tender peas.

Cavalier – maincrop pea that produces large crops, with good resistance to mildew.

MANGETOUT PEAS

Sugar Snap – thick fleshy pods, tall variety with robust growth. Excellent flavour with sweet stringless pods.

Oregon Sugar Pod – tall variety that tolerates poor soil and bad weather. Excellently flavoured mangetout pea.

PLANTING

Sowing seed

- Prepare a planting bed in autumn or winter and dig in garden compost to a depth of 20-30cm.
- From March to June when the soil is at least 5°C, make a 5cm deep drill with a hoe. Sow the peas about10cm apart, spacing the rows 46cm apart. Rake back the soil and firm down with the back of the rake. Water in.
- If possible, cover the rows with curved cages of chicken wire netting to prevent birds from digging up the seeds and seedlings.

DIGGING IN COMPOST TO PREPARE FOR PLANTING.

Where to plant

Chose a site in full to partial sun, as peas enjoy warm conditions. Dig in plenty of compost before planting, working well into the soil for good drainage.

SOWING PEA SEEDS IN ROWS.

Special care

When the young plants are 7-10cm tall, push tall twigs with branches into the soil to provide supports, or erect a trellis or wire frame from posts, about 2m high and tie pea netting to the stakes. Train the tendrils around the supports or netting to secure.

IN SEASON

Spring

For a longer harvesting time, plant several rows two weeks apart.

RIGHT: PLACING STICKS OR TWIGS IN THE SOIL FOR THE PEAS TO GROW UP.

Summer

Stake plants with branches or trellis and pea netting for support and easier picking. Keep well weeded.

When plants begin to flower, keep well-watered or the pods may not form fully.

Autumn/Winter

After harvesting, cut the stems back to the ground, but leave the root nodules in place. Dig them into the soil next spring, as this will enrich the soil with nitrogen.

PICKING AND STORING

- Gather peas young, as soon as they are well filled, to encourage the production of more pods. Peas left to mature on the plant, will stop it flowering and fruiting.
- Pick just before they are needed and store in the refrigerator in their pods, or shell them and store in a plastic bag for up to 3 days.
- Freeze peas on the day of picking.
- Pick mange tout or sugar snap peas with scissors when they are young and the peas are just forming in the pods.

PESTS AND DISEASES

Birds and mice can be a problem, so cover crops with netting to prevent them being eaten.

Pea thrips feed on the developing pods, making them distorted and silvery. Spray with derris or pyrethrum.

Pea moth can be a problem. Spraying with permethrin 10 days after the first flowers form, can help combat this.

POTATO – Solanum tuberosum

- Annual
- Height 35cm
- Spread 1-1.5m

Potatoes are an easy crop to grow and there are so many varieties all different in size, colour, texture and flavour. The skin may be red, yellow, purple or white and the flesh creamy, yellow or mottled. Textures can be waxy or floury, so choose varieties that suit your culinary needs and the growing conditions in your area.

Potatoes are classified as 'first early', 'second early' and 'maincrop' varieties. Plant early crops in late March for lifting in July, or grow second earlies for harvesting in August. Main crop potatoes can be planted from late April for harvesting in September.

Apart from their enormous value as a food crop, potatoes are a valuable crop to grow on land that has become infested with perennial weeds which are difficult to eradicate. After growing, lifting the crop and manuring, the soil will be in good condition for growing other vegetables next season.

VARIETIES

First early

Arran Pilot – high yields of white-skinned medium sized tubers. Good resistance to scab.

Epicure – round, white-skinned tubers. Hardier than most early varieties even in cold sites.

Concorde – heavy cropping, very early. Large oval tubers with pale yellow flesh. Good resistance to late frosts.

Second early

Maris Piper – a prolific cropper with a white skin, waxy flesh and creamy flavour.

Wilja – high yielding, long white tubers with pale yellow waxy flesh. Good disease resistance and excellent for cooking.

Estima – heavy cropper with pale white skin and yellow flesh. Great for chipped potatoes.

Maincrop

Desiree – heavy crops of pink skinned tubers with yellow flesh. Good texture and flavour and versatile in cooking.

King Edward – high yielding, good quality crop, but susceptible to blight. Good for baking.

Maxine – round, smooth, red skinned tubers with white flesh. Remains firm when cooked.

DESIREE

Salad potatoes

Belle de Fontenay – yellow kidney shaped tubers, with a waxy texture and a good flavour for salads.

Pink Fir apple – pink skinned, irregular shaped long tubers, with excellent flavour and texture for salads.

PUT SPROUTING TUBERS IN A WOODEN TRAY OR EGG BOXES.

PLANTING

Sowing seed potatoes

- In late February or six weeks before planting, set out seed potatoes in egg boxes or wooden trays, with the eyes uppermost. Leave in a frost-free place until several shoots 1cm long appear; this will increase the yield of the crop.

- In spring, fork over the ground and rake in a general fertiliser. In March to April, dig 15cm deep drills 60cm apart.
- Place the seed potatoes in the drills at 46cm intervals with the sprouted 'eyes' at the top.
- Using a hoe, draw up the soil to cover the drills, making a 15cm high mound over the planted rows.

Where to plant

A site with full sun will produce good growth and crops. Well-drained moist soil, rich in organic matter is best and a pH of between 5.08 and 6.0 is best to help avoid potato scab.

Special care

- As the foliage grows, rake the soil up over the rows to form a ridge. Earth up when the stems are about 20cm high. Break up the soil between the rows and use a hoe to pile the earth against the stems to make a ridge about 30cm high.
- Keep the soil moist in dry weather and do not allow the soil to dry out once the tubers have formed.
- In warm humid conditions, spray the surfaces with a fungicide to help control potato blight.

POTATOES IN ROW

IN SEASON

Spring

Chit the potatoes in trays before planting out. Plant out 4 weeks before the last frost.

Summer

Earth up the rows to exclude light from the crop. Water and weed regularly.
Harvest early crops.

Autumn

Harvest crops when the foliage turns yellow and dies back. Leave crops in the ground until late November, unless there is danger of severe frosts.

PICKING AND STORING

- Dig 25cm away from the row. Lift the tubers with a large fork taking care to keep it away from the plant. The tubers spread out and are easily damaged by careless lifting. Lift on a dry day and leave in the sun for a few hours to dry out before storing.
- Store the harvested potatoes in a dark, cool dry place. Light will make the tubers turn green, so store in trays or sacks and cover with sacking to exclude light.

DIGGING UP POTATOES

PESTS AND DISEASES

Potato blight is a fungal disease that thrives in warm, humid conditions from July. Yellow blotches on the leaves and white fungal growth underneath the leaves, indicates potato blight. Later the whole plant turns brown and the tubers are damaged and sunken areas appear. Regular spraying at 10 day intervals with Bordeaux mixture will control when the weather is humid.

Scab attacks the tubers and appears as rough, scab-like spots. Scab is worse in alkaline soils and regular watering is a good deterrent.

PUMPKIN
~ Curcubito maxima

- Annual
- Height 60cm
- Spread 2.5m

The fruits of this species are grouped according to their shape and size. The three main types being miniature, sweet and giant. Pumpkins are versatile, and the flesh can be eaten as a vegetable, or baked into a pie filling. The sweet, stringless pumpkins are best for this use. Pumpkins need a long growing season, so seed is best started indoors.

VARIETIES

Baby Bear – trailing, miniature orange fruits 12cm wide. Very tasty flesh.

Atlantic Giant – giant pumpkin that can produce huge prize winning fruits.

Triple Treat – bright orange-skinned, very sweet tasty flesh. Edible seeds.

PLANTING

Sowing seed indoors
If the soil is below 13°C, grow indoors in pots. Sow three seeds in peat pots filled with John Innes No.1 potting compost. Push the seeds down into the compost and leave them in a warm light place to germinate.

Where to plant
Pumpkins flourish in low humidity and some will tolerate cooler conditions. Full sun and moderate rich, well-drained soil is necessary for a good crop. Making a special raised bed, enriched with compost will allow deep root growth.

Planting the seedlings

- After five to six weeks the plants should have produced three to four true leaves. Only plant out when all danger of frost is over. Warming the soil with fleece will help give the plants a good start.
- Depending on the variety, make planting holes 1.5m-7m apart, a spade's width and depth. Fill the hole with organic compost, or well-rotted manure. Replace the soil to form a raised mound then water well. Thin out the seedlings, leaving the strongest one in each pot. Plant in each raised mound and firm in the soil.

SEEDLINGS WITH LEAVES.

- Placing a sheet of black plastic sheeting over the mound and planting through this will warm the soil, suppress weeds and keep the soil moist. This will also protect the fruit from contact with the soil.
- If the weather is cool or variable, cover with horticultural fleece until the weather improves. Water the plants weekly and feed with a general fertiliser every two weeks.

Special care

- For a good harvest, fertilise the female flowers with a male flower. Female flowers have a small fruit at the base. Tap the pollen from the male flower, which has a slender stem, onto the centre of the female flower.
- Place the maturing fruits on a plank of wood, plastic sheeting, bricks, or roof tiles to protect against rot and pests.
- Give each pumpkin a quarter turn each week to keep all the sides round in shape.
- For giant pumpkins, direct all the plant's energy into a single fruit by removing all but one fruit per vine.

IN SEASON

Spring

Grow seed indoors; soak it overnight first to help germination. Sow in peat pots late March to April.

Summer

Transplant seedlings with care, as the roots can be easily damaged. Water regularly and feed with liquid seaweed extract.

Autumn

Pinch out the growing tips. Support the fruit on a surface away from the soil, such as plastic or wood.

Winter

Pick and store before the first frosts.

PICKING AND STORING

Pick the fruits when they are fully coloured and have a hollow sound when tapped. Allow the skins to harden in the sun before storage. Store the larger fruits carefully in a frost-free shed.

PESTS AND DISEASES

Protect new seedlings from attacks by slugs and snails.
Mice will nibble the developing fruits, so protect the area with thorny twigs.

TURNING THE FRUITS EACH WEEK GIVES A GOOD SHAPE.

RADISH
~ Raphanus sativus

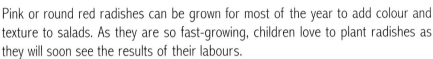

- Annual
- Height 8-20cm
- Spread 5-12

Pink or round red radishes can be grown for most of the year to add colour and texture to salads. As they are so fast-growing, children love to plant radishes as they will soon see the results of their labours.

Exotic varieties of radish, such as the Mooli or Daikon, belong to a group of long white radish which are used sliced or grated in Asian dishes; these types flourish in cooler temperatures. Seeds for more exotic varieties can be obtained from specialist seed merchants.

VARIETIES

Cherry Belle – fast-growing type with bright scarlet skin and mild-flavoured white flesh. Can be harvested three to four weeks after sowing.

French Breakfast – spring variety with a cylindrical shape; scarlet with white tops. Tender with a sweet mild flavour.

Scarlet Globe – a reliable old favourite, popular for its mild flavour and good quality. Can be sown under cover.

Long Black Spanish – winter variety with black skin and white flesh. Extremely hot. per bulb.

Mooli Type

April Cross – sweet, crisp, juicy and mild. Long white root grows to 45cm long with a 7cm diameter.

Long White Icicle – winter variety with long white root with tender flesh and a nutty flavour.

PLANTING

- Plant new rows of spring seed every eight to ten days for a continuous crop. Continue sowing from spring until the hot summer weather arrives. Sow winter crops from mid-late summer.

Where to plant

Do not dig in manure prior to sowing. Grow in rich soil that has been manured for a previous crop. Because radishes are in the ground for a relatively short period, they can be grown as a crop between rows of other vegetables that take longer to mature. Choose a sunny open site if possible.

Sowing seed

- In late February, break up the soil to a depth of 30cm and rake in a general fertiliser.
- In early March, mark out 2cm deep drills, spaced 30cm apart, with a hoe. Sow the seeds in groups of three, spaced at 15cm intervals. Cover the seed with soil and water in gently.

CHILDREN LOVE SOWING RADISH SEEDS.

Special care

- Thin out the seedlings after the first sets of leaves appear allowing 10cm between each plant. Keep well watered all season.

IN SEASON

Spring

Sow spring radish seed as soon as the soil has warmed. Plant new seed for continuous crops.

Summer

Sow winter radish seed from mid-late summer to mature before the cooler autumn weather slows down growth.

Autumn

Leave winter radish in the soil to mature.

PICKING AND STORING

Pull the radishes as required, when the roots are young and tender and 2cm in diameter. Pick and eat on the same day of harvesting. Don't leave spring radish in the soil for longer than ten weeks, or they will become tough and woody and will run to seed.

PESTS AND DISEASES

Flea beetles can be a problem and they will attack roots and eat holes in the leaves. Sowing seed early in the season avoids beetles. Dust infestations with derris.

RADISH IN THE GROUND READY FOR PICKING.

RHUBARB
~ Rheum x hybridum

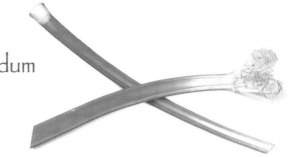

- Perennial
- Height 1.25
- Spread 1-1.25

The delicious red stalks of rhubarb are cooked and used more as a fruit, but this plant is actually classified as a vegetable. Rhubarb is easy to grow and one plant will provide up to ten years of produce. Rhubarb can be grown from seed, but for best results, lift and divide crowns, or buy virus-free plants from a nursery.

VARIETIES

Early Champagne – early type, with a sweeter flavour than most varieties. Produces long scarlet stalks, with a superb flavour. Good for winemaking.

Timperley Early – very early and suitable for forcing. Narrow stalks, variable in size, are red at the base and green at the top. Harvest from February onwards into late spring.

Victoria – a reliable old late variety, producing thick stalks from April to late into the summer. Heavy yielding.

Valentine – tender pale rose pink stalks, hardy with a delicious flavour for puddings and jams.

PLANTING

Because rhubarb will occupy the ground for up to 10 years, the ground must be well prepared.

Where to plant

Rhubarb thrives in full sun, in an open unshaded area. Rich deep fertile soil that has good drainage with a pH of 5.0–6.0 is ideal. The plant has deep roots, so ensure that a good deep layer of compost or well-rotted manure is dug in early.

Planting rhubarb sets

- In spring, dig a hole 50cm deep and 1m wide. Plant the sets 90cm apart and space rows 90-1.2m apart. Fill with layers of well-rotted compost and well-dug soil. Rake in a general-purpose fertiliser or bone meal.
- Spread the roots of the rhubarb set out into the hole, refill with soil and cover the crown with 5cm of soil, leaving the buds just below the soil. Firm in the soil and water thoroughly.

Special care

- When the leaves appear, mulch round the base of the plant with compost. Water in dry spells to keep the soil moist.
- Cut out any flowering shoots as they appear.

IN SEASON

Spring
Plant new sets in early spring.

Summer
Mulch and water regularly. Add a top dressing of general fertiliser or well-rotted manure in mid-summer.

Autumn
Cut out flowering shoots.

MULCHING ROUND THE PLANTS TO KEEP IN MOISTURE.

Winter
Divide the roots of established plants into sets, making sure each piece has at least one bud. Lift the crown and divide into sets with a spade or knife. Each set should be about 10cm wide with plenty of roots. Pack into pots of potting compost for three months to establish before planting out in spring.

140

PICKING AND STORING

- Don't harvest new plants for the first 12-18 months after planting. Pick only a few sticks from each plant in the second year.
- Twist stalks off by grasping near the base and twisting upwards, or cut with a sharp knife, being careful not to cut into the crown. Do not over pick, as this will weaken the plant. Use immediately or chop into cubes and open freeze on a tray, then pack into polythene bags when frozen solid.

PESTS AND DISEASES

Crown rot damages buds and makes the stems thin. Dig out and burn infected plants and do not replant in the area.

ABOVE: TWISTING OR CUTTING AWAY THE PINK STALKS TO HARVEST, AVOIDING THE CROWN.

LEFT: GROWING PLANT WITH LEAVES.

SALAD CROPS

LETTUCE – Lactuca sativa

- Annual

Home-grown lettuce require little effort and there is no comparison to the flavour and crisp texture of a freshly cut lettuce from your vegetable plot.

There are two types of lettuce, those that produce hearts, and non-hearting lettuces that produce a mass of foliage.

VARIETIES

LETTUCE HEART

Head or cabbage lettuce

All the Year Round – butterhead lettuce with tasty, compact, soft green leaves.

Little Gem – compact and sweet flavoured. Small and quick to mature, Good for smaller plots.

Webbs Wonderful – large hearted, crisp, tender and reliable. Slow to bolt even in dry weather. Lasts well when fully grown to maturity.

Buttercrunch – large American variety with a creamy and very crunchy heart. When mature, stands for a long time without bolting.

Lakeland – an Iceberg type of crisphead that produces tight, crisp green leaves. Reliable even in poor summers.

Lobjoit's Green – dark green, tall growing Cos lettuce. Tasty old variety with large crisp leaves: can be subject to tip burn.

THE ALLOTMENT GARDENER

Loose-leaf lettuce

These are non-hearting lettuces, which produce curled foliage that can be picked over a period of time; the plants will continue to grow and produce further leaves for picking.

Lollo Blonda – fresh pale green leaves. Frilly ball-shaped plants excellent in salads.

Salad Bowl – bright green, crisp and tender deeply lobed loose leaves. Good resistance to bolting.

Oak Leaf – loose leaves in several colours, from pale green to light brown.

Red Salad Bowl – curly dark bronze green to burgundy leaves. Lasts well if picked regularly; good for small plots. Good contrast in salad leaf mixtures.

Ruby – crinkled and pale green with deep red tints. Good resistance to heat.

Salad Bowl Mixed – masses of green deeply lobed crisp leaves. Good resistance to bolting.

OAK LEAF LETTUCE

LAND CRESS

PLANTING

Where to plant

Salad crops grow well in full sun, especially in spring and autumn. Summer crops will benefit from some afternoon shade. Lettuce prefers a well drained, slightly alkaline soil. More than any other crop, it requires a well-nourished soil, rich in humus. Incorporate plenty of well-rotted manure, organic compost, or old mushroom compost, in the preceding autumn.

Sowing indoors

In early spring sow seed thinly in trays or modules scattering on the surface of moist potting compost. Leave uncovered in a light cool place. Thin out, leaving the strongest seedlings, then harden off gradually before planting out in rows in fine, well dug soil.

Sowing seed outdoors

- From April to mid May make drills 1cm deep, spaced 30cm apart. Place seeds 1cm apart in the drills. Barely cover the seed with soil and firm in. Water in gently.
- Thin seedlings out regularly as they develop. If late frosts occur, protect the seedlings with horticultural fleece. Water regularly and mulch to keep the soil moist.

PICKING AND STORING

- In late May to late June, harvest non-hearting lettuce by cutting the leaves off near ground level, leaving a stump to re-grow. After 2 weeks the crop should have started to re-grow from the stumps and a fresh crop of leaves should be available in another one to two weeks.
- Harvest dense hearted lettuce when the heads reach full size and feel firm and dense. Harvest early in the morning when the moisture level in the leaves is at its highest. Refrigerate immediately after cutting.

PESTS AND DISEASES

Protect plants from rabbits with a chicken wire fence or cover.

Slugs and snails will damage seedlings and eat mature leaves. Remove slugs by hand at night or with a biological slug control. Surrounding the plants with gravel or crushed eggshells will make a scratchy texture that will discourage them.

LETTUCE SEEDLINGS IN ROWS.

CORN SALAD
~ Valerianella locusta

- Annual

These tasty leaves, sometimes know as lamb's lettuce, Mache, or lambs' tongues can be eaten all year round. As they are packed with vitamin C, beta-carotene and folic acid, they also provide a good boost to aid a healthy diet in winter.

VARIETIES

Cavallo – has deep green leaves and crops heavily throughout winter and spring.
Jade – robust summer variety that is tender and mildew-resistant.

Verte de Cambrai – a very hardy traditional French variety with small leaves and a good flavour. Crops throughout winter and spring.

Grote Noordhollaindaise – very hardy and robust variety that tolerates cold. Crops throughout winter and spring as a 'cut and come again' crop.

PLANTING

Where to plant
Corn salad is a hardy, robust plant that will flourish in a sheltered position with full sun or light shade. It tolerates most soils with good drainage but fertile, moisture-retentive soil will produce best results.

Planting and growing
- In spring, rake in a general-purpose, slow-release fertiliser and sow seed thinly in drills as for lettuce.
- The seedlings will be very slow growing in the early stages, and then growth will suddenly speed up.
- Thin the seedlings when they have four leaves, into spaces 8cm apart.
- Extra seedlings can be transplanted for growing between rows of other taller crops.

PICKING AND STORING

Harvest once the leaves are 5-7cm long. Cut a few leaves from several plants. Do not weaken by removing too many leaves at once, which is particularly important during the winter months.

PESTS AND DISEASES

Corn salad is a fairly trouble-free crop, but birds may be a nuisance. Make a zig-zagged frame on low sticks with cotton thread to keep them off the crop.

ENDIVE – Cichorium endiva

- Annual

Endive is also known as Escarole, Frisee, Batavia or Grumolo. There are two types of endive – curly-leaved and broad-leaved. Endive is often blanched by tying the darker outer leaves up over the inner leaves, to encourage the milder tasting creamy leaves in the centre. Endive makes a delicious salad mixed with other leaves, or enjoy the crisp, nutty, slightly bitter flavour on its own, tossed with olive oil and hot grilled bacon lardons.

VARIETIES

Moss Curled – produces compact heads of dark green fringed leaves. Withstands both heat and frost. Crops late autumn into winter.

Riecia Pancalieri – very curly white tinged ribs with rose tinged mid ribs. Bolt resistant. Crops summer, autumn or winter.

Tres Fine Maraichere – finely cut curled leaves with a delicious, mild, nutty flavour. Grows well in moist soils. Crops in autumn.

Broad leaved Batavian – is a tightly packed escarole with larger, broad dark green leaves with a creamy yellow heart. Crops in autumn.

PLANTING

Where to plant

Plant in an open site. Spring crops will thrive in full sun, but summer crops will need partial shade. Plant in rich, moist fertile soil to encourage rapid growth.

Planting and growing

- From late March to August, sow thinly in drills 1cm deep, spaced 30cm apart.
- When the first true leaves appear, thin out the seedlings leaving spaces of 23cm in between them.
- Water regularly. Avoid using nitrogen-rich fertiliser, as this will cause the leaves to rot.
- To blanch the plants, make sure the leaves are completely dry and tie around the outer leaves with raffia, bringing them up over the inner leaves. Cover each plant with a large flowerpot to block out the light; leave a gap at the base for ventilation. The heads will be ready in 2-3 weeks.

CURLY ENDIVE LEAVES

PICKING AND STORING

Harvest about seven weeks after sowing, when the plants are 20cm in diameter. Pick off individual leaves or cut with a sharp knife about 3cm above the soil to encourage the plants to re-sprout. Use immediately or store in a plastic bag in the fridge for up to three days.

PESTS AND DISEASES

Slugs are the main problem. Pick these off by hand. Keep the plants well watered and mulched to prevent tip burn.

RADICCHIO – Cichorium intybus

- Annual

This colourful salad leaf is a form of chicory and comes in two varieties.

VARIETIES

Treviso – a tall-leaved plant that resembles cos lettuce. It has a loose head and white or green inner leaves. As the temperature cools, the colour changes from red to purple.

Choggia or round radicchio – produces closely packed round heads with red leaves with white veins.

PLANTING

Where to plant
- Plant in an open position in full sun or partial shade. Rich, well-manured moist soil is best.

Planting and growing
- Prepare a well composted seed bed. Sow seed in drills 1cm deep and 30cm apart.
- Thin out when the first true leaves appear to space 20cm apart. Water to keep the soil moist and mulch around the plants to retain moisture.

PICKING AND STORING

Cut the heads from the roots at soil level; the roots may produce new, smaller heads. For leafy varieties, pick a few leaves when needed. Store heads in a plastic bag with damp kitchen paper and store in the salad drawer of the fridge for up to one week.

PESTS AND DISEASES

Leaf rot can affect the crops in cold weather. If the outer leaves turn brown and slimy, peel these away. Leaving larger spaces between the plants will give good air circulation and may prevent this condition.

ROCKET – Eruca vesicaria

- Annual

Rocket is a popular Mediterranean salad plant and is actually a member of the cabbage family. It adds a peppery flavour to salads and may be called rucola, roquette, or erugala. The plants mature in 4-12 weeks, but will soon run to seed, so frequent sowings are needed for a constant supply.

PLANTING

Where to plant
- A sheltered shaded position is best and any moderately fertile, moist soil will produce this crop.

Planting and growing
- Sow in 1cm deep drills spacing the rows 20cm apart. Rake back the soil and water well.
- When plants have two true leaves, thin out the seedlings and use in salads. Plant a further row of seeds at this stage.

PICKING AND STORING

Pick the leaves when they are young and tender. Regular picking will encourage new growth, as long as some leaves are left remaining on the plant. Remove any seed heads before they develop fully as these will stop growth.

PESTS AND DISEASES

Slugs and snails are the main problem. Remove these by hand.

SPINACH ~ Spinacia oleracea

- Annual
- Height 10-15cm
- Spread 20cm

Spinach is a hardy, easy to grow vegetable and its edible leaves are highly nutritious cooked, or eaten raw in salads. Although expensive to buy in the shops, you will find a row of home-grown spinach costs just pennies and it will continue cropping for many months. Traditionally, spinach was divided into summer and winter varieties, but many modern seed varieties are now dual purpose.

VARIETIES

Long Standing Round – a summer variety of Savoy leaf spinach with tasty leaves. Tolerant of cold and slow to bolt, it crops over a long period.

Medania – summer variety, smooth green leaves, vigorous growth and slow to bolt. Withstands hot dry weather and mildew resistant.

Dominant – for spring and summer sowing, good all rounder with thick leaves. Good resistance to bolting.

Giant Winter – late autumn/winter variety, good disease resistance and will withstand some frost.

Other varieties

New Zealand – good for dry soils. Not a true spinach, but a good substitute. Small soft fleshy leaves with a mild flavour. Crops well and very hardy.

Perpetual (spinach beet) – very hardy, providing summer and winter crops and will not bolt in first season. Soft tender leaves and stems.

PLANTING

Where to plant
Spinach is very sensitive to day length and early sowings should be in sunny sites. Summer sowings should be in partial shade to help prevent bolting. Spinach needs well-drained rich, deeply dug soil. If the soil has bad drainage, grow in raised beds.

Preparing the bed
In winter, double dig the soil and incorporate well-rotted compost to help retain moisture. Rake and level.

Sowing seed
- From spring to autumn, sow seed every three weeks, 15cm apart in drills 2cm deep, spaced 30cm apart. Lightly rake back the soil.
- When the seedlings grow, thin out to 15cm apart if they begin to touch each other. The thinnings can be eaten in salads. Water well in dry weather and keep down weeds by hoeing.

SOWING A NEW ROW OF SEEDS IN THE SHADE OF TALLER CROPS.

Special care
Protect early and late sowings from cold weather by covering with horticultural fleece or cloches.

IN SEASON

Spring
Sow seed for summer crops in a sheltered site. Sow new plantings every three weeks for continuous cropping.

Summer

Pick regularly to prolong cropping. Pick off any flower heads to keep the leaves growing. Water regularly.

Autumn

Sow for winter harvest.

Winter

Prepare ground for next spring.

PICKING AND STORING

Treat spinach as a 'cut and come again' vegetable. Cut the leaves when small, young and tender. Remove the leaves 2.5cm above the ground and allow the plant to re-sprout. Cut the leaves away carefully with scissors. or pick off by hand. Use the leaves fresh, or store in the refrigerator for one to two days in a plastic bag.

PESTS AND DISEASES

Downy mildew can be a problem, so look for resistant seeds. Leaving wider spaces between the plants can be of benefit.

- Bolting, or going to seed is a common problem, particularly in hot summers.
  Planting summer crops in shade will prolong the harvest.

SPINACH PLANT

SQUASH - Curcubita pepo

- Annual
- Height 0.5-1m
- Spread up to 3m

Summer squash are bushy, and the green training bushes have a creeping habit. These will spread, so allow plenty of room for them. They come in vivid colours, in several shapes and can provide a highly ornamental addition to the kitchen in autumn. As well as being decorative, they have a nutty tasting flesh that is delicious served hot, roasted in cubes.

VARIETIES

Custard White – scalloped patty pan type flattened white fruits. Compact bushy habit suitable for smaller plots.

Golden Nugget – early maturing bush type that produces round orange fruits.

Yellow Crookneck – curved yellow fruits with a firm flesh and good texture.

Sweet Dumpling – vigorous trailing plant with small fruits with creamy skin and flesh.

Early butternut – trailing, dark green-skinned fruits with bright orange flesh. Grows and matures rapidly and the fruits store well.

PLANTING

Planting in mounds

- Make planting holes 0.5-1m apart a spade's width and depth. Fill the hole with organic compost or well-rotted manure.
  Replace the soil to form a raised mound, water well and cover with grass clippings if available.
- Sow two–three seeds 2cm deep in each mound. When the seedlings have three true leaves, thin out to leave one plant in each mound.

Where to plant

Choose a site in full sun, with good air circulation and plenty of room for the plants to spread. Rich fertile soil will produce the best results. Dig in organic matter before planting. To keep out pests, cover the mounds with cloches or horticultural fleece until the flowers form, then remove to allow the bees to pollinate.

Planting pot-grown seedlings

- Sow seed in peat pots of compost indoors, or in greenhouses in mid to late spring. From mid-May onwards, transplant in the peat pots when the danger of frosts is past. Plant in mounds as above, and mulch around each mound.

Special care

- From mid-May onwards, keep well watered. Trailing types can be trained over canes on the ground, or up trellis to support the fruits. Support individual fruits where necessary.
- In June, pinch out the tips of the main shoots of trailing varieties when they are 60cm long and train them evenly around each plant.
- Hand pollinate if the weather is cold early in the season. Remove a male pollen-releasing flower and dust into a newly opened female flower, or paint on to the female with a fine paintbrush.

HUGE SQUASH BEING HARVESTED

IN SEASON

Spring

Sow seed indoors in April in peat pots. In May, sow seed outdoors or transplant pot-grown plants.

Summer

Water and feed well. Mulch with straw to conserve water.

Autumn

Stake or tie fruits onto trellis to support the fruits.

PICKING AND STORING

When the fruits are ripe, cut from the plant with a sharp knife. Ripe fruits will have a hollow ring when tapped. Do not allow them to grow too large as they will become tough with little flavour. If storing for a few months, allow the fruits to stand in the sun to harden the skins.

PESTS AND DISEASES

Summer squash may develop a rot in wet weather and wither at the blossom end. Remove the fruits and apply a liquid feed, if the leaves are still healthy. If the rot develops to the stem, destroy the plant.

SQUASH RIPENING ON THE VINE.

THE ALLOTMENT GARDENER

SWISS CHARD
- Beta vulgaris ssp. cica

- Hardy biennial
- Height 40cm-1m
- Spread 40-70cm

This fast-growing vegetable produces delicate spinach-like leaves. They are slightly more peppery in flavour and the tasty mid-ribs can be chopped and sauted separately. This vigorous and heavy-cropping vegetable is high in sodium, potassium, iron and beta-carotene. The broad dark green leaves can have white, crimson red or shocking pink ribs, which add dramatic colour to the vegetable plot.

VARIETIES

Fordhook Giant – thick pale green stalks with huge glossy green leaves with white veins and ribs. High yielding with good flavour.

Luculus – pale yellow green leaves with slender creamy stalks. Crops heavily and tolerant to bolting.

Bright Lights – delicate, dark green leaves with highly coloured stems in shades of pink, orange, gold and violet.

Rhubarb Chard – bright crimson stems with dark green puckered leaves. Prone to bolting after a spring frost.

PLANTING

Where to plant
Choose a site in full sun or partial shade with fertile, moisture retentive soil. The pH should be neutral to slightly alkaline and acid soils may need lime adding.

Planting broad beans
Dig over the soil and incorporate a 5cm layer of compost into the soil four weeks before the last spring frost. Rake over.

Sowing seed

- Swiss chard seeds are multigerm or clustered seeds. Sow thinly 10cm apart in drills 1.5 deep.
- When the plants are 15cm high, thin out every alternate plant leaving spaces 20-30cm apart.

Special care

Water plants regularly in hot weather; keep weed free and mulch with organic matter such as grass clippings. Apply a liquid fertiliser to give the plants a boost.

IN SEASON

Spring

Dig over the bed adding compost or a general-purpose fertiliser.

Summer

Thin out seedlings and water well. Keep down weeds and mulch.

Autumn

Harvest the outer leaves, to encourage regrowth.

MULCHING THE PLANTS WITH GRASS CUTTINGS KEEPS SOIL MOIST AND DETERS WEEDS.

HARVESTING — CUTTING AWAY THE OUTER LEAVES

PICKING AND STORING

Harvest the outer leaves regularly. Cut them away with a sharp knife and leave the inner shoots to develop. Continue to pick to promote new growth and treat as a 'cut and come again' crop. Use on the day of picking as the leaves will begin to wilt. Cut the stems away from the leaf part and cook these separately. The leaves will take three to four minutes to cook, as for spinach and the stems eight to ten minutes, chopped, steamed or braised.

PESTS AND DISEASES

Brown patches may appear on the leaves which can be fungal leaf spots. Remove and destroy the affected leaves.

SWEDE – Brassica napus
Napobrassica Group

- Annual
- Height 25cm
- Spread 35cm

Swedes are a long season crop and can take 20–26 weeks to mature, but the sweet flavour of this root vegetable is delicious. The root contains small amounts of vitamins B and C,and is low in calories and carbohydrates.

VARIETIES

Best of All – medium-sized globes with purple skin and yellow flesh. Hardy and reliable crop that can stay in the soil all winter.

Marian – globe-shaped variety with delicious, sweet yellow flesh. High-yielding with good disease resistance.

Ruby – dark purple skin with creamy flesh that darkens to orange on cooking. Large globes with excellent flavour. Winter hardy with good resistance to mildew.

PLANTING

Where to plant
Choose a site open to full sun and remember that this crop will take up space for a long time. Do not grow swede on the same plot for two years in succession. Any fertile, non-acid soil is suitable; swedes prefer a pH of 5.5–7.0, so very acid soil needs liming. If possible, use land manured from a previous crop and do not dig in fresh compost, as this can give forked roots.

Sowing seed
- In spring or early summer, rake a general -purpose fertiliser into a prepared seedbed.

DRILL FOR SWEDE SEEDS

- Make 2cm deep drills spaced 35cm apart. If the soil is dry, lightly water first.
- Sow the seed very thinly, and then gently rake back the soil to cover.

Special care

- As soon as the seedlings produce their first pairs of leaves and are about 2.5cm high, thin out to spaces of 20cm apart. Firm back the soil after thinning.
- Weed around the growing plants by hand and water thoroughly in dry weather to prevent the swedes turning woody.

IN SEASON

Spring
Sow in early May to late May.

Summer
Weed and water regularly.

Autumn
Begin harvesting or leave in the ground until needed.

Winter
Lift and store crops before severe weather.

TOP: SOWING SWEDE SEEDS.
ABOVE: COVERING SWEDE SEEDS

PICKING AND STORING

When the leaves have turned yellow, lift as needed. Ease the roots up with a fork. Store unpeeled for up to 5 days in a cool place. To store the whole winter crop, lift and layer in boxes of sand or peat substitute.

PESTS AND DISEASES

Swedes are prone to club root, which is a problem on poorly drained acid soil. Powdery mildew can be a problem, appearing as a white powder on stems and leaves and will cause stunted growth. This is a problem when plants are dry at the roots. Dusting the seedlings with derris or pyrethrum provides an organic answer to pests and insects.

SWEETCORN

~ Zea mays

- Annual
- Height 1-3m
- Spread 30-70cm

Freshly picked sweet corn, cooked dripping with butter, is a true delight.
Home grown corn kernels are available in a variety of sizes and vary from white to pale yellow in colour. Avoid buying the super sweet hybrids if you live in a cool area and choose one of the special varieties recommended for colder summers.

VARIETIES

Sundance – good for cooler areas. Sweet sugary flavour with creamy yellow kernels.

Golden Bantam – early variety with tasty golden cobs. Hardy and grows to 180cm. Good for freezing.

Earliking – very early, large cobs with good sweet taste. Strong plants, good for cooler areas.

Minor – Baby sweet corn to pick immature when 7m long. Good for stir-fries.

PLANTING

Where to plant
A light, well-drained fertile soil, slightly acid, with a pH of 5.6-7.0 is desirable. As the plants need a long growing season, the site should be open, sunny and warm and sheltered from cold winds and frost. As sweet corn is wind-pollinated, the plants are best grown in a square or block setting.

Sowing seed indoors

- Better germination will be achieved by sowing in pots or modules of compost.
- Before planting, place seeds on the surface of moistened kitchen paper on a tray or plastic container. Cover with a lid and put in a warm place.
- After 2-3 days sow each seed in peat pots or modules filled with compost.
- Keep in a heated greenhouse or a warm windowsill until the dwarf plants appear.
- Harden off outside, gradually, once there is no danger of frost.

Planting the seedlings

- The seedlings will be sensitive to disturbance and root damage, so handle carefully, or plant the peat pots complete.
- In late May, dig holes with a trowel and plant the sweet corn seedlings in a block 30-46cm apart, each way. Water regularly.

Special care

- Use a hoe to draw soil over the roots that appear on the surface, but as sweet corn is shallow-rooted, avoid touching or damaging the roots.

WATER SMALL PLANTS REGULARLY.

- Stake and tie in the plants in windy, exposed areas.
- Mulch the soil with straw to conserve moisture and keep down weeds. Apply a nitrogenous liquid feed when the cobs start to swell.

IN SEASON

Spring

Sow seed under cover indoors.

Spring/Summer

Harden off and transplant seedlings.

Autumn

Harvest crops. Use the dead stalks and husks for composting.

PICKING AND STORING

- The cobs are ready to harvest when the silks wither and turn dark brown.
- Test if the ears are ripe, peel away the outer leaves and push your thumbnail into a grain. If the liquid runs clear, it is unripe; if it is milky it is ready to pick.
- To pick, hold the ear near the base and twist off the plant in a downward motion.
- Eat or freeze within 24 hours of picking, as the sugars in the ears will turn to starch and the sweet flavour lost. To freeze, blanch in boiling water for four minutes, cool in cold water, drain and pack singly in foil, then plastic bags.

TWISTING AWAY THE EARS WHEN THE SILKS (END TUFTS) TURN DARK — HOLD THE EAR NEAR THE BASE AND TWIST DOWNWARDS.

ABOVE: EAR OF CORN

LEFT: ROW OF TALL SWEET CORN PLANTS.

PESTS AND DISEASES

- Smut can appear as large galls on cobs and stalks in hot dry summers. Cut these off and burn immediately and do not grow sweet corn on the same site for three years.
- Fruit fly maggots can bore into the growing tips of seedlings producing deformed leaves and stunted growth. Using 'dressed' seed and a granular insecticide can help prevent this.

SWEET PEPPER
~ Capsicum annum

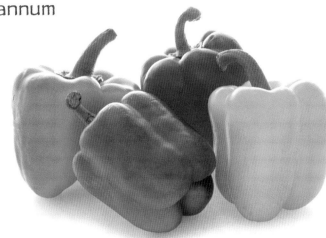

- Annual
- Height 50-90cm
- Spread 60-70cm

Home grown sweet peppers have an excellent flavour and texture and are available in many shapes and colours, not normally found in the shops. Peppers start out green before ripening, but will mature to colours in a range from red, orange, green, gold, purple and even black. Sweet peppers are related to the tomato plant and require similar growing conditions.

VARIETIES

New Ace – high yielding, bright red fruits, early cropping. Good for cooler areas.

Luteus – yellow fruits, early cropping. Thick walled fruits.

Big Bertha – excellent for cooler areas. Large green bell pepper, can grow to 10cm wide by 18cm long. Mild-flavoured and good for stuffing.

Sweet Chocolate – unusual chocolate brown fruits. Good for freezing.

Ariane – fast-growing, heavy crops of bright orange fruits. Thick walled fruits with crisp flesh, good for salads.

THE ALLOTMENT GARDENER

PLANTING

Propagating sweet pepper seeds

- Sow indoors in late spring in trays of moist seed compost. Cover thinly with compost then cover with glass and newspaper. Turn the glass daily.
- When three true leaves appear, transplant into 6cm peat pots.

SWEET BLACK PEPPER.

Where to plant

For outdoor growing, a sunny sheltered site is vital; otherwise grow under glass, cloches or clear plastic sheeting. Light, fertile, moisture-retaining soil will give best results.

Planting the seedlings

- Harden off the young plants and plant outside under cloches, or transplant into 23cm pots of compost or growing bags. Protect with plastic sheeting, cloches or glass. Water well, especially in dry weather.
- Provide cane supports for the plants as they grow.

Special care

- Remove the first flowers and feed with a dilute liquid fertiliser weekly, throughout the growing season.

PEPPER IN GROW BAG.

SWEET BELL PEPPER

IN SEASON

Spring
Sow under cover. Transplant the seedlings when the danger of frost is over.

Summer
Keep weed-free and water regularly. Harvest regularly to encourage longer cropping.

PICKING AND STORING

- Do not let the first set of fruits mature on the plant. For the best yield, pick the first set of peppers when they are green and the skin is smooth and glossy and they are the size of a tennis ball; this will make the plant produce more fruit with a higher yield. Allow the next set of fruits to mature and ripen.
- Cut the fruit off the plant at mid stem, with a sharp knife, leaving a short stem attached to the fruit.
- Don't pull or break the fruits from the stem as this can cause damage and stop the plant from fruiting.

PESTS AND DISEASES

Outdoor pepper plants are usually disease free. Check for aphids and red spider mite, which can be found on the underside of leaves, which turn mottled and brown.

OPPOSITE: STAKING THE PLANTS
WITH BAMBOO TO HELP
SUPPORT THE FRUIT.

ROMANO PEPPER.

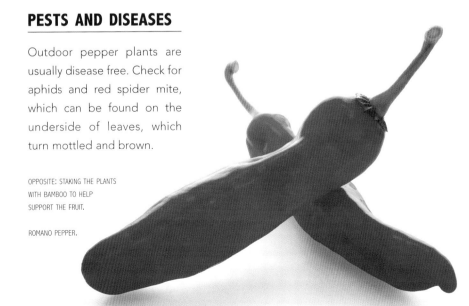

THE ALLOTMENT GARDENER

TOMATO
~ Lycopersicon esculentum

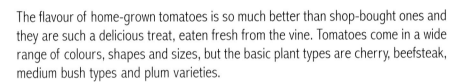

- Annual
- Height 0.25-1.25m
- Spread 0.5-1m

The flavour of home-grown tomatoes is so much better than shop-bought ones and they are such a delicious treat, eaten fresh from the vine. Tomatoes come in a wide range of colours, shapes and sizes, but the basic plant types are cherry, beefsteak, medium bush types and plum varieties.

VARIETIES

Cherry

Mirabelle – extra juicy miniature fruits with a sharp, tangy flavour. Orange-yellow fruits can produce over 60 trusses on one plant.

Tumbling Tom – very sturdy plants with crops of heavy tasty fruits. Good disease resistance.

Gardener's Delight – produces long trusses with large numbers of very sweet cherry tomatoes over a long period.

Medium

Moneymaker – a traditional old variety with delicious, scarlet fruits, succulent and full of flavour. Tall, resilient, heavy cropping plants.

Shirley – good quality tasty and tender fruits. Good for cooler temperatures and produces an early crop. Resilient and good for organic growing.

Tigerella – tasty red and yellow striped fruits with a rich flavour. Crops well over a long period.

Beefsteak

Marmande Super – tall stocky plants with an early crop. Deep red ribbed fruits with a delicious full flavour. Good for slicing.

Dombito – good disease resistance, tall stocky plants with delicious large heavy fruits.

Super Beefsteak – is an old variety with huge fleshy fruits. Fruits can be 400g in weight and need extra support. Good for stuffing and slicing.

Plum

Olivade – heavy cropping with a good texture and flavour for cooking.

Roma VF – good outdoor bush plum variety, crops heavily and needs good support. Good for cooking as puree, soups and sauces.

PLANTING

Sowing seed indoors

- Sow seed thinly in trays of potting compost eight weeks before planting. Cover with 3mm of compost and water lightly. Cover with a sheet of glass and newspaper and keep in a greenhouse or on a sunny windowsill. Turn the glass daily.
- When the seedlings emerge, transfer to peat pots filled with potting compost. Make holes in the compost large enough to take the seedlings.
- Water well and keep in a light, well-ventilated place. Thin out any extra seedlings from each pot and harden off when the danger of frost is over.
- Plant out when the first pairs of true leaves appear just above soil level.

POT-GROWN TOMATO PLANT.

Where to plant

Plant outdoors in a site open to full sun, but protected from wind. A spot against a south-facing wall is ideal. Plant in full draining soil, previously enriched with compost, or in growing-bags or containers full of moist compost.

Planting out

- Plant out pot-grown tomatoes after the last frost once the roots have filled the pot and the first flower buds appear. Water the soil or growing bags well before planting.
- Insert stakes near to the plant and tie in the plants as they grow, training them vertically with soft string, or loose plastic ties.

PINCHING OUT THE SIDE SHOOTS AND TOP.

Special care

- Pinch out the side shoots while still small on tall or cordon varieties. Leave some side shoots to develop on bush or trailing varieties. Pinch out the top shoot on taller varieties when four trusses have set.
- Keep the soil constantly moist but not waterlogged. Feed with a liquid tomato fertiliser according to the manufacturer's instructions. Overfeeding and watering can weaken and reduce the flavour.

IN SEASON

Spring

Sow indoors in March to April. Transplant seedlings when two pairs of true leaves appear. Harden off before planting out.

Summer

Plant out when the danger of last frosts is over. Provide stake supports. Water and feed.

Autumn

Harvest.

PICKING AND STORING

- Pick ripe fruit regularly by hand when they are fully coloured. Hold the tomato in your palm and break off the fruit at the raised joint swelling on the flower stalk.
- At the end of the season, pick all the unripe fruit and place them in one layer on a tray. Put a ripe apple or pear in the middle and the ethylene gas emitted will help ripen the tomatoes naturally.

PESTS AND DISEASES

Blossom end rot appears as a hard brown flattened patch at the end of the fruit. This indicates calcium deficiency and is usually caused by erratic watering. Fruit can also split in hot weather as a result of variable watering. If growing in grow bags, watering and feeding must be regular and methodical.

PICKING THE TRUSSES.

UNUSUAL VARIETIES.

TURNIP – Brassica rapa var. rapa

- Annual
- Height 25cm
- Spread 25cm

Turnips are one of the easiest vegetables to grow. They are tasty to eat and the turnip top leaves are delicious. The roots may be flat, round, or long, and the flesh white or yellow. They are best eaten young when they have a fresh, peppery flavour, but can be stored for later use.

VARIETIES

Purple Top Milan – early variety, flat shaped and purple reddish top with white flesh. Sweet and tender flesh and matures very quickly.

Tokyo Cross – F1 hybrid with small tasty white globes. Matures rapidly in 30-40 days. Good late summer to early autumn crop.

Golden Ball – Yellow flesh with good tasty flavour. Sow in late August. Hardy and good for winter storing.

Manchester Market – green topped globe variety skin and white flesh. Good for winter storage.

PLANTING

Where to plant

Choose an open site with fertile, well-drained soil. Summer turnips need to be grown rapidly, and early varieties need shelter from winds. Cool moist conditions are preferred with a pH of at least 6.8, and plenty of organic matter worked into the soil.

Sowing seed

- Sow early turnips in February-March. Prepare a seed bed, removing stones and raking smooth. Do not dig deeply and add lime to acid soil.
- Mark out 2cm deep drill 30cm apart. Sow the seed thinly and then rake back the soil and water in gently.

Special care

- The seedlings will grow very quickly, so thin them when they reach 2.5cm height. Leave 10cm spaces between for early crops and 20cm for main winter crops.
- Water regularly and do not let the soil dry out or the roots will turn dry and woody.

IN SEASON

TURNIP SEEDLING

Spring

Sow early varieties outdoors in spring. In colder areas, cover with horticultural fleece. Thin out seedlings and sow new rows for continuous cropping.

Summer

Harvest early varieties. Sow maincrop in July to August and thin out to 20cm.

Autumn

Weed and water regularly. Harvest maincrop from September onwards.

PICKING AND STORING

Harvest early varieties when they are young and tender. Gather up when they grow to the size of a golf ball and pull by hand like radishes. Ease up later varieties of larger turnips with a fork to prevent damage. Keep in a cool place and use within a few days. Alternatively, twist off the leaves of main crop varieties and store in a box in a cool shed in between layers of peat substitute.

PESTS AND DISEASES

Flea beetles are 3mm long with black and yellow stripes. They will nibble holes in the leaves and stunt the growth. A large infestation can kill all the young plants. Sow in early March to miss the first attacks and keep well watered to help resist attack.

Herb Crops

Herbs are some of the easiest crops to grow on your plot, and will be successful as long as they are planted in the correct place. Some herbs love the sun, but others need shade to protect them and keep their delicate leaves tender. Herbs can be divided into three groups – annuals, evergreen and herbaceous.

Evergreen herbs include bay, sage, thyme and rosemary and this group will tolerate both heat and drought as they are mainly of Mediterranean origin. All this group need to flourish in a poor or average soil, are good drainage and plenty of sun.

Herbaceous herbs include the perennials that will die down each year and appear again in the next spring. This group includes chives and mint and these should be treated as border plants and cut down each autumn, when they die back for the winter.

Annual herbs need to be sown in pots in the spring and planted out when the soil is warm enough. These include basil, chervil, dill, marjoram and parsley.

BAY – laurus nobilis

- Evergreen

Bay is a small, attractive evergreen tree grown for its aromatic leaves. It is usually grown in containers but can be grown in open soil, where it can reach a great height if left unchecked.

GROWING

This herb needs a site in full sun with some protection from winds. An average well-drained plot will be adequate, as this herb does not need a rich soil.

CARE

Buy young but well-established plants and protect in very harsh weather to prevent the leaves from browning.

HARVESTING

Cut the young leaves and use fresh, or dry and store in a dark place to keep the colour of the leaves.

SAGE – salvia

- Perennial

This evergreen shrub will thrive in even the poorest of soils. There are numerous varieties of sage with coloured variegated leaves, but the common varieties with grey green foliage are the most hardy. The fragrant foliage is attractive in summer, with the flowers adding dashes of blue or scarlet colour.

GROWING

Sage needs full sun and a well drained, light soil and will grow well in containers. Seeds can be sown indoors in spring in pots of compost, or cuttings can be propagated by taking a small piece of softwood cutting with a mature shoot attached in autumn.

CARE

Prune after flowering to encourage new growth. Sage can retard the growth of other plants so do not plant near annuals such as cucumbers.

HARVESTING

Pick leaves before the plant flowers to use fresh or for drying. Dry the leaves on a wire rack in a well-ventilated area. Store in dry, airtight containers in a cool dark place for use in savoury dishes.

THYME ~ *thymus*

- Perennial

The dainty leaves and delicate pink or purple flowers create a herb that is full of fragrance. There are numerous species of thyme, each with different features and colourings. Planting contrasting plants can provide an ornamental feature that is also useful in the kitchen.

GROWING

Thyme is a Mediterranean herb that needs a well drained, warm sunny site. Most thymes are hardy with some half-hardy. Take softwood cuttings in spring and summer and grow on in pots for a good supply of plants.

CARE

Trim the bushes after flowering to avoid straggly plants and encourage new growth.

HARVESTING

Pick the sprigs during the growing season for using fresh, or tie sprigs together in bunches and hang upside down to dry.

THE ALLOTMENT GARDENER

ROSEMARY – rosmarinus officinalis

- Perennial

This popular herb has evergreen aromatic needles with a fine aroma. It is available in upright varieties that grow as a bushy shrub, or as prostrate rosemary, that is more suited to slopes or containers but can also be used for ground cover.

GROWING

Rosemary is vulnerable to low temperatures or exposed areas, especially when the plants are young. Plant outdoors after danger of frost is past, in a sunny site with well-drained soil. If planting in containers, add material for good drainage, such as perlite. If soil becomes too wet, roots may rot in winter.

CARE

Prune regularly. Keep young plants pinched out to encourage a bushy habit. Softwood cuttings will root easily in pots or directly into the soil to establish new plants.

HARVESTING

Cut tender sprigs in early summer as leaves become tougher in late summer. Use fresh, dry upside down in bunches, or use frozen in ice cubes.

CHIVES
~ Allium schoenoprasum

- Perennial

This hardy perennial herb is small and delicately flavoured. Chives will produce grass like clumps of hollow dark green leaves that are topped by clusters of delicate lilac flowers in summer. This is one of the most versatile herbs and as it has a mild onion like flavour it is good sprinkled over hot savoury dishes, omelettes and egg dishes, in soups or salads.

GROWING

Chives need plenty of light and thrive in full sun. Plant them as a border plant in the vegetable patch in well-drained soil.

CARE

Feeding is not needed. Water regularly and cut the leaves regularly to ensure a continual supply. Divide the clumps every two or three years. Dig up a clump, tease it apart and spread out the roots, then replant as smaller patches.

HARVESTING

Cut the long leaves with scissors about 5cm above the soil level. Don't cut away all of the leaves, then the plant will re-grow.

MINT - Mentha spp.

- Perennial

This vigorous perennial herb is part of large group with many varied forms each with a distinctive fragrance and flavour, ranging from peppermint to lemon, spearmint, ginger and pineapple mint. It is a hardy upright herb, which will spread rapidly if left unconfined.

GROWING

Mint will thrive in a sunny position but can tolerate partial shade. Keep the soil moist in summer. Mints are invasive and can be as troublesome as weeds if allowed to get out of hand. Restrict root growth by planting in a sunken container such as a large pot or old bucket at least 30cm deep. Fill with compost or garden soil and plant the pot in a hole with the rim above the soil.

CARE

Every 3-4 years, dig up the pot, discard the central clump and replant a healthy piece from the outer edge.

HARVESTING

Cut 30cm long stems before they flower to use a fresh herb. Freezing is more successful with mint than drying, which loses the powerful flavour.

TOP: PIPERITA

MIDDLE: PULEGIUM

BOTTOM: SPICATA

BASIL – ocimum basilicum

- Annual

The foliage of this tender annual has a wonderful fragrance and a distinctive clove like flavour, which adds zest to savoury dishes, particularly those with tomatoes.

GROWING

Basil requires an open sunny site in well-drained moist soil. As basil thrives in rich soil, dig in leaf mould, or well rotted compost or manure before planting. Sow seeds under glass or indoors on a sunny windowsill, then harden off before planting. Plant out after the risk of frost is over.

CARE

Pinch out the tips to make the plant bushy. If slugs are a problem, spread a fine layer of grit or crushed eggshells around the plants to deter them.

HARVESTING

Pick the leaves every week or so to keep the plant from flowering and promote more leaves. Basil cannot be dried or frozen and must be used freshly.

CHERVIL - Anthriscus cerefolium

- Annual

Chervil is a tender herb with decorative leaves that are similar to parsley. It has a tendency to self-seed.

GROWING

Chervil grows best in partial shade, as it will run to seed in full sun. Sow directly into moist, rich soil in early spring to mid-summer. Thin out the seedlings after three weeks, then put in a repeat sowing for a good supply of the herb.

CARE

Water well in dry weather. Remove the flower heads if you do not want the plant to self-seed.

HARVESTING

This herb grows quickly, so the tender young leaves can be picked about nine weeks after sowing. Pick the leaves young and use in delicate egg dishes or in salads. Chervil cannot be dried, but can be frozen.

183

DILL - Anethum graveolens

- Annual

Dill is a fragrant herb with feathery leaves and seeds grown for its mild but distinctive flavour. An upright herb with a height of up to 1 metre, dill will reseed every year so choose a permanent spot when planting.

GROWING

Dill thrives in moist well drained soil in a sunny position. The seeds will germinate even in cool weather. Thin out plants to 20cm apart when large enough to handle. Make successive plantings in rows from spring to summer in rows 60cm apart.

CARE

Keep plants well watered. Avoid planting near fennel plants as they are so similar, they may cross breed and lose their distinctive qualities. Insects love the flowers of dill, so plant among vegetables.

HARVESTING

Clip the foliage throughout the growing season. To save the seeds, cut off the seed heads and hang upside down in paper bags to dry out and collect the seeds. Use the seeds in pickling or in vinegars, and the leaves for flavouring soups, salads and fish dishes.

MARJORAM - Origanum spp

- Perennial

Marjoram is available in two varieties. Pot marjoram or oregano is usually used dried, and sweet marjoram has a more delicate flavour and is best used fresh.

Many Italian dishes rely on the delicious fresh flavour of this herb as used in pizzas, tomato and meat dishes.

GROWING

Marjoram is a Mediterranean herb and thrives in full sun. Soil must be well drained but can be of poor to average quality. Sow the seeds in spring into plugs or trays of compost. Thin out seedlings and prick out into pots, then plant out.

CARE

Before the plants die down for winter, cut back the year's growth. Protect pot-grown varieties in winter to preserve the plant for the following year. Divide clumps in spring or autumn and replant immediately for new growth.

HARVESTING

Marjoram has a finer, stronger flavour just before flowering. Cut the stems just above the lowest set of leaves. Use fresh, frozen or dry upside down in bunches on a hot summer's day.

PARSLEY - Petroselinum crispum

- Biennial

Parsley is probably the best known of the culinary herbs and is easy to grow and care for. Parsley will grow from spring into autumn in its first year and continue into the following year. There are two main varieties: plain or flat-leaved French and Italian types, which are more strongly flavoured, and the decorative, curly leaf type with frilled leaves and a milder flavour.

GROWING

Parsley grows best on fertile well-drained soil in a shady or part shaded position. Sow seeds in modules or trays of compost in spring and transplant when the seedlings are 3-5cm tall. Alternatively, plant seed directly outdoors 2-4 weeks before the last frost. Germination is slow and may take several weeks.

CARE

If birds are a problem, cover the seedlings with horticultural fleece. Thin the plants out and water during dry periods.

HARVESTING

Harvest until flowers open in the second year of growth. Using scissors, cut single leaves or bunches low down on the stems. Use fresh or can be frozen.

EXOTIC HERBS

CORIANDER
~ Coriandrum sativum

- Annual

This tender annual has scalloped leaves with a unique strong aromatic scent and spicy, fresh flavour. The leaves are used in curries and oriental dishes. The seeds have a spicy orange flavour and can be dried and used in savoury dishes or for pickling.

GROWING

Grow from seed directly into the soil in shallow drills, spacing the rows 23cm apart. Germination will be quicker if sown under glass or plastic. As the seedlings have long taproots, growing in seed trays is not successful and the seedlings will not transplant well.

CARE

Grow in a light, well-drained soil in a dry, sunny position. Coriander is difficult to grow in damp or humid conditions and does best in a hot dry summer. When the plants reach maturity, stake them for support.

HARVESTING

Pick leaves when young, tender and bright green. Cut the seed heads as they ripen and hang upside down, tied in bunches, covered loosely with paper bags. Dry out for ten days and shake the seeds into the bags. Store in airtight tins in a cool dark place.

THAI BASIL

~ Ocimum basilicum 'Horapha'

* Annual

Thai basils have purple leaves a marvellous rich scent and a rich aniseed flavour that form the base of many vegetable curries and spicy Thai and Asian dishes.

GROWING

Sow from seed directly into plugs or pots of compost in early spring. As the plant has long roots and will not transplant well, don't plant in seed trays. Position in a sheltered position with full sun.

CARE

Water regularly every evening and do not let the plants dry out.

HARVESTING

Pick the leaves young from the top of the plant to encourage new growth. Use fresh to enjoy the unique spicy flavour in stir-fries and Thai dishes.

THE ALLOTMENT GARDENER

LEMON GRASS
– Cymbopogon citratus

- Perennial

Lemon grass is a strongly scented tender grass with cane-like stems that are used grated or chopped as a flavouring in Asian dishes.

GROWING

As this herb originates from warm countries, it needs a moderately humid atmosphere such as a greenhouse or protected container or grown from seed in a heated propagating tray. Plant bought stems of lemon grass in pots of compost if they have a root left on them.

CARE

Keep in a humid environment in moisture retaining soil. If growing in pots, cover with a large loose fitting plastic bag with ventilation holes, or a moulded plastic bell-shaped cover.

HARVESTING

Cut the stems at ground level as needed.

Fruit Crops

Watching plants burst into blossom and then bear fruit that ripens in the sun's warmth appeals to the senses, as does the incomparable flavour and aroma of fresh, home-grown fruit. Delicious fruits, ripe for picking, are so rewarding, but many people believe you need a huge plot for fruit crops. You will be surprised how little space a few bushes take up, strawberries can be grown in pots and dwarf fruit trees will flourish in a small spaces or tubs. With so many crops to choose from, do make sure you include some on your plot.

APPLE - Malus

- Tree
- Height 1.8–8m
- Spread 1.5–8m

Apples can be grown in a variety of ways, ranging from great, spreading free-standing trees for large spaces, to the new dwarf columnar varieties which are ideal for allotments and small plots of land. An apple tree can bear fruit a year after planting, depending on the variety, and some will continue fruiting for up to 50 years.

Apples grow best in milder areas where spring frosts are rare. Pollination is essential for fruit to set, but some apple varieties cannot pollinate themselves. So, check before buying for a suitable partner to plant nearby; you will need another variety which flowers at approximately the same time, enabling cross-pollination to take place. Ornamental crab-apple trees can be good pollination partners.

VARIETIES

There are hundreds of varieties of apples to choose from at nurseries and from catalogues, but read the descriptions carefully to see if the variety is right for your plot and decide whether you want to grow for cooking or eating.

Apple varieties for eating:

Discovery – for picking in August. Good for a small garden, excellent flavour.

James Grieve – for picking early September with soft, juicy tangy fruits.

Jonagold – for picking mid October. A heavy cropping tree with a crisp fresh flavour.

Cox's Orange Pippin – for picking in October. Sharp tangy fresh flavour.

Sunset – for picking mid October. Similar flavour to Cox and a heavy cropper that stores well.

Apple varieties for cooking:

Bramley's seedling – for picking mid-October. Finest flavour and texture for cooking and a heavy cropper. This will establish into a very large tree.

Rev.W. Wilks – for picking early September. Large fruits with an excellent flavour. A compact tree that yields every other year.

Blenheim Orange – for picking early October. Good nutty flavour and a heavy cropper.

PLANTING

How to plant an apple tree:

- Prune the roots, cutting off any long or broken roots.
- Measure the root spread and dig a hole 7-10cm wider than this and as deep as the mark left by the soil on the tree stem.
- Fork over the soil in the hole and mix with compost to form a mound. Spread the roots over the mound so that the original soil mark on the stem is level with the soil surface.
- Place a stake in the planting hole 7cm away from the tree, taking care not to damage the roots. Tap the stake in to a depth of 30cm to give support to the tree.

STAKING AN APPLE TREE

- Work the soil and compost together amongst the roots and gradually fill the hole. Firm down the tree and water well.
- Tie the tree to the stake with plastic or rubber webbing tree-ties. The tie should have a spacer that fits between the tree and the stake to prevent the bark from chafing.
- Fit the tie just below the lowest branch. Loosen the tie as the trunk grows and thickens to prevent the tie from cutting into the tree, which could cause damage.
- Three years after planting, start to feed the apple tree every spring. Apply a general fertiliser on the ground under the canopy of the tree. Top up with organic mulch about 8cm thick over the same area.
- Established trees will not need watering, but during a prolonged drought, water every couple of weeks to ensure the crop of apples is not affected.

TYING A NEW TREE TO SUPPORT AGAINST WIND DAMAGE.

Buying a tree

When buying, look for guaranteed disease-free trees, which should be accompanied by a certificate. Avoid dry-looking bare-rooted trees, or those with large roots growing through containers. Choose a tree that will grow to a size to suit your garden and don't buy a large tree if you have a small garden.

Where to plant

Choose a sheltered site in full sun if possible. A south-facing site with well-drained soil, near a sunny wall is ideal. Prepare the soil well with plenty of well-rotted manure or compost. Apples will grow best in deep, well prepared, fertile soil and this will ensure a high fruit yield for many years. If you are growing more than one tree, you will need to space the trees according to their expected eventual size, according to their rootstock. Dwarf rootstocks can be planted 1.5 metres apart while larger trees with vigorous rootstocks should be planted up to 7 metres apart.

IN SEASON

Spring

Container-grown fruit trees can be planted at any time of year, but they will establish more quickly if planted in the spring or autumn when the soil is moist and warm. Prune out any dead or diseased branches and cut back overcrowded shoots or branches that cross each other. Apply fertiliser.

Summer

Thin the crop when the tiny fruitlets are about the size of large peas. Leave one apple from each cluster.

Autumn

Harvest the crop and store in trays.

TOP: FRUITLET FORMING ON THE BRANCH.
ABOVE: APPLE BLOSSOM.

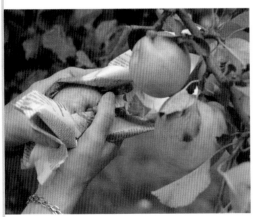

WRAPPING AND STORING APPLES INDIVIDUALLY IN NEWSPAPER FOR WINTER STORAGE.

PICKING AND STORING

Test for ripeness by holding an apple and twisting gently. If the fruit and stalk come away easily, the apples are ready to harvest. Pick the fruits carefully to avoid bruising and store only undamaged fruits. Wrap each apple in screws of paper so that the individual fruits do not touch. Store in one layer in a shallow moulded paper tray or wooden box in a cool dry place. The length of storage depends on the variety.

PESTS AND DISEASES

If you find dark green or brown spots on the fruit and leaves, or have disfigured fruit with blistered twigs and cracked surfaces, this is Scab. Scab is a fungus, so leaves need to be raked up and destroyed and scabby twigs should be pruned away. Spray with carbendazim three times up to the end of flowering.

APRICOT
~ Prunus armeniaca

- Tree
- Height 2-4m
- Spread 2.4m

Growing apricots is a challenge in cooler climates, but most varieties are winter hardy and outdoor cultivation is possible if you have a warm spot with full sun. A good crop will be produced when the spring is mild and you can provide a sheltered southern facing site with protection from frosts. Growing under glass is much more reliable, but pot grown plants will give lower yields of fruit than outdoor plants.

VARIETIES

Moorpark – for picking in late August. This popular variety has large fruits with a rich, sweet flavour. If conditions are frost-free, this is a regular cropper.

Alfred – for picking July-August. Smaller fruits than Moorpark with juicy, sweet rich-flavoured fruits. This variety tends to produce a biennial crop.

Farmingdale – for picking in late July. This American variety has earned a good reputation in Britain. The medium-sized fruits crop early and have an excellent flavour. It crops heavily and has some resistance to die-back.

New Large Early – for picking July–August. Large, oval fruits with a rich pale juicy flesh. Robust and hardy with good disease resistance.

PLANTING

Buying a tree

Buy two-three year old bare-rooted trees and look for those that have been trained into a fan shape, if they are to grow against a wall. Look for vigorous plants and avoid any that look stunted or show any signs of disease.

197

Where to plant

Full sun is necessary for fruiting, so place the tree against a sunny wall in a frost-free southern-facing site. Apricots are best planted in a rich, slightly alkaline soil that is well drained, but they will tolerate a variety of conditions. Mulch around the tree with a thick layer of organic compost and in hot weather, water regularly to keep the soil moist.

How to plant an apricot tree

- Measure the container that the tree is in and dig a hole of the same size. If the tree is bare-rooted, make sure the hole is wide enough to fit all the roots in without breaking them.
- Spread the tree roots out in the hole. Position a stake into the soil close to the tree, avoiding the roots. Fill the hole with soil and organic compost mixed together, then firm down the topsoil and water well.
- Hammer the stake into the ground firmly, then secure the tree stem to it with a rubber tree tie to prevent the wind from loosening the plant.

Training the plant into a fan

- If you buy a partly trained three-year-old tree with eight or more branches, these should be attached to wires on the wall and trained out into a fan. Tie each branch to a bamboo cane, placed in the ground at 45-degree angles. Spread out the canes to form a well-shaped fan and tie to the wires. In February, prune back each branch by about one third back to a bud, and then more branches will develop. Tie in the pruned branches firmly.
- If you are starting from scratch with a maiden seedling, after planting, cut back the main stem to just above the first bud. Attach supporting wires to a wall. Tie in two bamboo canes to the wires at 45-degree angles. The following summer, select two side shoots and tie them into the canes as they grow. Remove all other side shoots. The following summer, remove the canes and tie in the branches to the lowest horizontal wires attached to the wall. Tie in another pair of canes at 45-degree angles and attach two new shoots. Repeat the process every year until a fan shaped tree is established, pruning to remove any new or unwanted shoots.

PRUNING

199

IN SEASON

Spring

Prune the trees early while they are still dormant. Cut back all shoots by one third and pinch out the tops of all one-year old shoots.

Place hessian or netting over the bush in early spring to protect the blossom from frost damage. Remove during the day and support the net to keep it away from the flowers to avoid damaging them.

Apricots are self-fertile, but you can hand pollinate when the tree blossoms in early spring. Dab the buds with a ball of cotton wool from the time the buds open, to the time the petals fall.

Summer

To produce large fruits, thin out the developing fruits and pick off the smallest and most crowded ones when they are the size of a small cherry.

Water regularly in dry weather and do not let the soil dry out. This is especially important for newly planted trees. Harvest when the fruits come away easily from the tree, pick by hand, being careful to treat the fruit gently.

PICKING AND STORING

Pick the fruits by hand when ripened to a golden orange colour but still firm. The fruits should be easy to pull away from the stem, but handle them gently as the fruit can bruise easily. Keep the fruits indoors for a day before eating. If you have a glut, lay the fruits in a single layer in a tissue-lined box and store for one to two weeks in a cool dark place.

PESTS AND DISEASES

Generally, apricot trees are more disease-resistant than other fruit trees. Red spider mite and aphids are the most common pests, but you can control these by spraying the leaves with diluted washing up detergent.

BLACKBERRY - Rubus

- Perennial
- Height 1-2m
- Spread 1-4 m

Once you have established a blackberry hedge, you will have bumper crops of delicious juicy black fruits for years to come. Blackberries are vigorous, hardy perennial cane fruits belonging to the genus Rubus and are exceptionally spiny. These fruits are good for freezing, jams and jellies, desserts such as tarts and puddings, and for winemaking.

VARIETIES

Ashton Cross – for picking August to September. Thorny, wiry stems which yield a very heavy crop. A true wild bramble flavour and these berries are the best for freezing.

Loch Ness – for picking late August. The stems of this plant are thornless and erect, requiring little support. The fruit has a medium flavour with a heavy crop.

Fantasia – for picking in early September. These thorny bushes have vigorous growth. The fruit is exceptionally large, over 2.5m across.

PLANTING

Buying a plant
Buy a certified guaranteed disease-free plant from a reputable nursery. Look for strong healthy canes and avoid those with spotted or discoloured leaves. If buying bare-rooted plants, avoid those with dried out roots.

Where to plant

Blackberries prefer well-drained deep loam soil, but will establish in most soil types. Blackberries are easy to grow, but need shelter from strong winds and will need to be tied to training wires on stakes or trellis. The best yields of fruit are from bushes in sunny open sites.

Planting a blackberry bush

- Soak both bare-rooted and container-grown plants in water for four hours before planting.
- Dig a hole large enough for the root ball and enrich the soil with a layer of garden compost. Spread out the roots, loosely cover with soil, and water well.
- After planting, cut the canes down to a bud about 20cm above the ground. Apply a 5cm mulch of compost or manure. Tie shoots in to wires.

IN SEASON

Spring

Scatter a handful of fertiliser such as Growmore, around the base of each plant. Tie in new shoots to the wire supports. Cut away any weak straggly stems.

Summer/Autumn

Remove any unwanted suckers as they appear. Pinch out the growing tips when the canes fill the wires to encourage larger berries. After fruiting, prune out the old stems right down to the ground.

Winter

Prune the side shoots from the canes after the plant has stopped growing in the winter.

PRUNING — PULL OFF UNWANTED SUCKERS WHEN THEY APPEAR.

PICKING AND STORING

When the fruits are fully coloured and soft, pull each blackberry away from the stem. Pick on a dry day, as wet fruit will soon start to go mouldy. Use or freeze as soon as possible after picking.

PRUNING

You can control the shape and size of the bush by pruning back the tops of the canes to the height you want. Do this every year and the plant will become bushier and will bear more fruit with each successive season.

PESTS AND DISEASES

Blackberries are usually pest-free, but raspberry beetles may cause damage to the buds and their larvae will bore into the fruit. Spray with an insecticide before the buds open and again, when the petals have dropped.

BLACKBERRIES WILL RIPEN IN DIFFERENT STAGES.

BLACKCURRANT
~ Ribes nigrum

- Perennial
- Height 1.5m
- Spread 1-2m

You won't need a large garden to grow a few currant bushes. They are easy to grow and provide a delicious summer harvest rich in vitamin C. Enjoy them in tarts, puddings and pies, or make delicious blackcurrant jams and jellies. Currants freeze well, so store some away to enjoy in the winter months.

VARIETIES

Traditional varieties of blackcurrants are grown for their flavour, but these may not produce a crop every year. Modern varieties have been developed that flower in late spring and have the advantage of producing a reliable harvest every year, but these do not have such a distinctive blackcurrant flavour.

Baldwin – for picking late July-August. A traditional and popular variety. Compact in growth, the medium-sized berries hang on the bush long after ripening without splitting.

Wellington XXX – for picking mid-July. A traditional variety that has a superior sweet and juicy flavour. Crops are heavy with tough skins. Growth is vigorous and the bush will spread.

Laxton's Giant – for picking late June. Very large sweet fruits. The bush is vigorous and will spread, so plant well apart.

Ben Nevis – for picking late July. A modern variety with medium well-flavoured berries. Tall upright bush, resistant to mildew and frost.

Malling Jet – for picking late July. Late flowering modern variety with long strings of small berries with a blander flavour. Vigorous bush too large for gardens.

Ben Lomond – for picking late July. This modern variety has very heavy yields of plump berries on short stems with a good tart flavour. Upright compact bushes.

PLANTING

Buying a plant

Buy two-year old bare-rooted plants with at least three shoots. Buy from a reputable supplier who sells certified stock that is virus free. Avoid plants with discoloured or spotted leaves, as these can be an indication of disease.

Where to plant

Plant in a sunny but sheltered site. As blackcurrants flower early and are prone to frost damage, avoid planting in exposed open sites or in frost hollows.

Planting a blackcurrant bush

- Plant blackcurrant bushes deeply, as new shoots will develop from the base. Cover the basal fork where the branches arise with soil and cut back all shoots to the second bud.
- Place mulch around the bushes after planting and renew this each spring with a thick layer of mulch such as garden compost or well-rotted manure.
- To raise plants from cuttings, prepare a planting bed by digging over the soil well.

MULCHING AROUND THE ROOTS HELPS STOP WEEDS FROM GROWING.

In autumn cut mature stems into 20cm lengths above and below a bud, and strip the leaves from the lower half. Put each of these cuttings into the prepared ground so that the top bud is exposed. Place the cuttings in rows, 15cm apart, firm in, then water well. Cover the plants with a layer of straw or black plastic sheeting with a hole for each cutting to grow through.

IN SEASON

Spring
In early spring broadcast 100g Growmore around each bush before mulching.

Summer
Apply a potassium-rich liquid feed in summer when the fruits begin to swell. Unless there is heavy rain, water the bushes once a week. Keep weeds under control and hoe carefully or hand-weed round each bush, being careful not to touch the roots.

PICKING AND STORING

The fruit is ripe about a week after it turns black. To pick the currants, cut off whole stems bearing fruit and strip them at the table with the tines of a fork. By this method you are pruning the bushes at the same time. Store currants in the refrigerator on the stalk for up to a week.

PESTS AND DISEASES

You may find powdery white or brown mould on the shoot tips. This will not affect the fruit in most cases, if you are growing resistant varieties. Leaf-curling midge can cause twisted or distorted shoot tips, so prune these away and destroy them.

Birds will be attracted to the ripening currants, so protect plants individually with netting or build a fruit cage over a large area of bushes.

RIPE BLACKCURRANTS.

BLUEBERRY
~ Vaccinium corymbosum

- Perennial
- Height 1-2 m
- Spread 75cm

Blueberries are becoming more popular because of their health-giving qualities, as these delicious berries are packed with antioxidants and essential vitamins. Eat them straight from the bush or bake them into pies, muffins and cookies to enjoy their sweet black sticky juices.

As they are acid-loving plants, they will need to be grown in ericatious compost or soil with a low pH content.

VARIETIES

Highbush Blueberry is the only type found in the UK and different cultivars can be purchased from specialist nurseries or by mail order. These vary in cropping times and in flavour.

Bluecrop – for picking in early August. This is the most popular variety with mild-flavoured fruit. It has upright stems with vigorous growth.

Erliblue – early picking in July. This hardy plant produces vigorous growth with a heavy crop.

Jersey – for picking in August. This hardy erect bush can be grown in a shrub border.

Herbert – picking late in August. These large berries are considered the finest in flavour. The bush has vigorous growth.

PLANTING

Buying a plant

Buy bare-rooted plants by mail order or from specialist garden centres. Look for three strong stems and no leaf growth. Avoid plants which look dried-out.

Where to plant

You can only grow blueberry bushes in well-drained acid soil, which has a pH level of 4–5.5. Before planting, check your soil's acidity with a soil test kit. If your soil is over 7.5pH, grow the bush in acid compost in a 40cm pot or tub.

The plants can tolerate partial shade, but if you find a site in full sun, the plant will thrive. Sunlight and shelter from winds will produce best results.

Planting a blueberry bush

- Prune away any long or damaged roots. Dig a hole twice the width and depth of the roots. Pile up the soil in the centre and mound the roots over this.
- Fill the hole with soil, firm in and water well. Mulch with rotted leaves, sawdust or acid compost.
- Don't water with tap water and use only lime-free rainwater.

TESTING FOR ACID SOIL.

1. SCOOP THE SOIL INTO A TEST TUBE.

2. SHAKE THE TUBE, THEN MEASURE AGAINST A PH SCALE.

3. MULCHING WITH ACID COMPOST

IN SEASON

Spring

Prune away any weak or dead stems. Prune back weaker older stems and growth at the base to ensure a good harvest. Feed with fish blood and bone meal or an ericatious fertiliser after the first year's growth.

Winter

Once the bush is two or three years old, prune it by thinning down older stems.

PICKING AND STORING

The fruit will not become sweet for three days after it has reached its dark colour, so leave the berries on the branches. Harvest the berries when they fall easily from the plant. They can be stored in the refrigerator for 1-2 weeks or open freeze well on trays.

PESTS AND DISEASES

Birds will be attracted to the ripening fruit, so cover the bushes with netting or a fruit cage.

Success with blueberries depends on the right soil conditions; if the leaves begin to yellow and the stems die back, the soil is too alkaline and the bush may die. Mix a small amount of moss peat with potassium sulphate, bone meal and sulphate of potash as a fertiliser or replant the bush in ericatious compost.

BLUEBERRY BUSH

HYBRID BERRIES
- Rubus hybrids

- Perennial
- Height 2m
- Spread 2-4m

These delicious berries are a cross between a raspberry and blackberry. The most popular are loganberries and tayberries with sweet tangy berries and rich purple red colours. They are delicious served fresh with cream, layered in rum pots with other soft fruits, made into jams or puddings, pies and desserts. Just one plant will give a good supply of berries and these will freeze very well on the day of picking.

VARIETIES

Loganberry Ly59 – for picking July-August. These canes are thorny but yield good crops of medium sized dark red fruits with a sharp and tangy flavour.

Tayberry Medina strain – for picking July-August. Large dark red sweet fruits. Not suitable for cold or exposed plots of land.

Thornless Boysenberry – crops July-August. These large purple berries are oblong in shape and have wild blackberry flavour.

PLANTING

Buying a plant
Buy in early spring and choose a virus-free certified plant. Buy bare-rooted plants with strong canes. Do not choose plants with dried out looking roots.

Where to plant
Plant in well-drained soil and enrich with garden compost at the time of planting. Hybrid berries need an open site with full sun and you will need to provide supports for the plants if the site is exposed to the wind.

Planting a bush

- Dig a hole larger than the root ball, then spread the roots out evenly in the hole. Fill the hole with soil, firm in by hand then water well.
- After planting, prune back to a bud 25cm above ground.
- Drive in stakes or posts to support the plant and attach four rows of wire at 30cm intervals.
- Attach the canes to the wires with string ties. Fan the canes out to encourage new growth.

Propagating new plants

Train the stems of existing plants along the ground in midsummer and pin them down to just behind a growing tip. Cover with 5cm of soil and in the next spring cut away the newly rooted section and transplant it.

IN SEASON

Spring

Feed the plants in early spring by broadcasting a general fertiliser such as Growmore using 35g per square metre around each plant.

Summer

Apply a mulch of compost or peat around the base of the plants to keep the soil moist and cool in summer and keep down the weeds.

All through the summer, train the new shoots off the ground and away from the fruiting canes.

Autumn

After the plants have fruited, cut out all the old canes that produced fruit that year, and attach new canes to the wires.

CUTTING BACK CANES AFTER FRUITING.

PICKING AND STORING

Pick on a dry day, as wet fruit will soon start to go mouldy. Harvest the fruits when they are fully ripe and will twist away from the stalk easily.

PESTS AND DISEASES

- Raspberry beetle may be a pest and the tiny white grubs can ruin the crop. If these are found on the crop, spray with liquid Derris when the petals have fallen.
- Remove any wild brambles from the area as they can spread disease.
- Birds will be attracted to the ripening fruit, so protect the plants by stretching netting over them.

LOGANBERRY PLANT.

CHERRIES
~ Prunus avium

- Tree
- Height 5m
- Spread 5m

Cherries are available in sweet dessert types in black, red and yellow varieties and are delicious for eating fresh. Acid cherries are sour and used for cooking and bottling.

VARIETIES

Stella – crops late July. A self-fertilising sweet cherry with large juicy red to dark red fruit. A good cropper with upright, vigorous growth and a spreading habit when established. A good choice for gardens or allotments.

Van – crops late July. Not suited for small plots or where space is limited, but the flavour of these sweet dark red cherries is superb. A reliable and heavy cropper with vigorous growth.

Morello – crops August. The most popular acid cherry. The fruit if picked when red, it is sour but if left until almost black, it becomes bitter-sweet. Growth is compact and spreading.

Merton Glory – crops late June. Superb large sweet yellow cherries with firm white flesh. A regular heavy cropper. Upright growth with a spreading habit.

PLANTING

Buying a cherry tree

Buy bare-rooted trees 1-1.5m in height with a trunk about 2cm thick. Choose self-fertile varieties bare-rooted trees need to be planted in autumn but container-grown trees can be planted at any time.

Where to plant

Cherry trees need a site that is open to lots of direct sunlight and protected from wind. Deep, free draining soil is best.

A NEW BARE-ROOTED PLANT.

Planting a cherry tree

- Dig a hole one and a half times as wide and twice as deep as the roots. Mix garden compost with some of the soil removed.
- Mound up the soil in the holed and spread the roots over the mound, making sure the base of the trunk is above ground.
- Without disturbing the roots, position a wooden stake in the mound 8cm from the tree.
- Fill the hole with soil and firm around the trunk and the stake. Tap the stake firmly into the soil.

A POT- GROWN CHERRY TREE.

IN SEASON

Spring

Drape netting over in spring to protect the blossom from frost damage but avoid damaging the blossom.

Summer

Water regularly in dry weather. Keeping the roots moist will prevent the fruit from splitting.

During the first four years of growth prune lightly to take away damaged branches and suckers.

Winter

Plant in November for next spring's crop.

PICKING AND STORING

Leave the cherries on the tree until they are ripe.

Harvest the fruit by cutting with scissors or secateurs. Cut off in bunches with the stalks attached. Eat or use immediately, particularly if the fruits are starting to crack.

CHERRIES RIPENING ON THE BRANCH.

PESTS AND DISEASES

Bacterial canker infection is initially shown by pale-edged leaf spots; affected branches will produce fewer leaves than normal and gum oozes out from the bark cankers. Treat by cutting out diseased cankers and apply fungicide paint around the wound.

Birds will be attracted to buds in early spring and summer to the ripening fruit, so cover the tree with netting for protection.

CURRANTS – RED & WHITE
– Ribes rubrum

- Height 1-2m
- Spread 1-2m

Red and white currants are the most attractive soft fruits with bunches of jewel-like berries hanging from the bushes in high summer. They are basically the same fruit with different colours and they make neat hedges in allotments and small plots. Currants are only on sale for a very short period in greengrocers', so growing your own gives you the opportunity to make delicious pies, jams, jellies and wines. They will also freeze exceedingly well in trusses, on the stems.

VARIETIES

Laxton's No.1 – crops mid-July. An old red variety with a vigorous upright bush that spreads slightly. Heavy crops of smaller sized fruits with good juice and flavour.

Redstart – crops mid August. A new red variety that is late cropping. Well-shaped bushes are upright with big yields of heavy cropping trusses.

White Grape – crops mid-July. Pale yellow-white berries have an excellent sweet flavour but a lower yield.

White Versailles – crops early July. A reliable cropper year after year with long heavy trusses of sweet, pale yellow fruits.

PLANTING

Buying a plant

Buy bare-rooted plants with two or three sturdy stems and no sign of leaf growth. Avoid plants that have shrivelled stems or a white powdery coating on the buds, indicating signs of disease.

Where to plant

Avoid frost pockets. Currant bushes will tolerate partial shade, but a sunny site is best. The bushes need well-drained soil for best results, so dig in plenty of organic compost to keep the soil moist and nourish the plants. Currant bushes thrive when their roots are not in direct hot sun, so apply a thick layer of mulch for protection.

If you want to grow fan-trained plants, position against a fence or wall and tie in to parallel horizontal wires at 60cm width about 120cm above ground level.

Planting cuttings in a bed

- In the autumn, dig over the planting bed and remove any weeds. If the soil is not well drained mix perlite granules into the top 30cm of soil.

FROM TOP: TAKING A CUTTING AFTER THE LEAVES
BEGIN TO FALL IN AUTUMN.
MIDDLE: PREPARING CURRANT CUTTING.
BOTTOM: PREPARING HOLE FOR CUTTING.

- After the leaves begin to fall, cut mature currant stems into 20cm lengths above and below a bud, stripping the leaves from the lower half.
- Place each cutting in the prepared bed 15cm apart, so that only the top bud is exposed. Firm the soil then water well.
- Cover the cuttings with a strip of black horticultural plastic and make a hole for each to grow through or cover with a 5cm layer of straw. Remove the plastic or straw in spring and water to keep the soil moist.

IN SEASON

Summer

Water each bush well once a week and mulch to conserve moisture. Prune away side shoots to four-five leaves from the base.

Winter

Plant new bushes. Prune any stems older than three years to the ground, as these will bear less fruit. Cut away any diseased wood or branches, crowding the centre to leave six sturdy stems.

FROM TOP: PLACE THE CUTTINGS INTO THE PREPARED GROUND.
CURRANT CUTTING IN GROUND.
COVER THE CUTTINGS WITH STRAW OVER THE WINTER MONTHS.

PICKING AND STORING

Snip off the trusses of fruit when the fruit is coloured and shiny. Not all the fruit will ripen at the same time, so pick over the bushes twice or three times to collect the ripe berries. Don't pick the currants singly but remove the whole cluster. Store in the refrigerator on the trusses for up to a week or freeze immediately. To remove the berries, hold the truss with one hand and pull through with the tines of a fork.

PESTS AND DISEASES

Birds are attracted to the bright red berries, so cover the bushes with netting as soon as the colour starts to develop.

HARVESTING THE TRUSSES OF FRUIT.

DAMSON

~ Prunus domestica ssp. instita

- Perennial
- Height 4-5m
- Spread 5m

These small trees are ideal for gardens and allotments and will produce a heavy crop of juicy small fruits packed with a tart, sweet and sour flavour. Damsons are the cultivated form of the wild plum or bullace, and a damson tree is very easy to look after, producing a heavy crop of fruit in the autumn. As damsons have a sharp flavour they need the addition of sugar in pies, crumbles and puddings. These dark purple fruits are especially suitable for making delicious jams and chutneys.

VARIETIES

Merryweather – for picking late September. This is the largest variety, with round, blue black fruits that crop heavily.

Prune or Shropshire Damson – for picking late September-October. Small oval blue-black fruits with yellow flesh and a regular, but moderate crop. A small upright tree, ideal where space is limited.

PLANTING

Planting
Buying a damson tree
Buy a bare-rooted tree in early autumn. Avoid trees less than two years old, as they will not bear fruit for several years. If space is limited, ask for a dwarfling rootstock.

Where to plant
Position the tree in a plot open to full sun. If you place it on the perimeter of the plot, it can also act as a windbreak. Avoid planting where the soil will be damp for long periods.

Planting a damson tree

- Prepare the soil by digging thoroughly, removing all weeds. Fork in a handful of general fertiliser.
- Dig a hole big enough to accommodate the roots when they are fully extended. Spread out the roots and position a stake in the hole.
- Plant the tree to the same depth it was in the nursery. Return the soil and firm in well. Tie the stake with a tree tie and water well.
- After planting, prune back any damaged branches and shoots. Prune back the main branches by a third to a good outward facing bud.

IN SEASON

Spring

Mulch the tree in early spring with compost. To encourage growth, spread an organic fertiliser around the base of the tree.

Summer

Prune away any broken or dead branches and cut away any suckers at the base of the tree.

DAMSON TREES PRODUCE HEAVY CROPS OF FRUIT.

SHRIVELLED FRUIT

Autumn

Leave the fruit on the tree for as long as possible to achieve a good flavour.

Winter

Prevent the onset of brown rot fungus by destroying any shrivelled fruit that has been left on the tree.

PICKING AND STORING

The heavy crops that are produced need picking while firm and well flavoured, but not soft. Use as soon as possible or spread out on trays in a single layer and refrigerate. Freeze the whole fruits for jam-making later; the skins will probably split on freezing, but this will not affect the jam.

PESTS AND DISEASES

- Silver leaf can affect the damson and appears as a silvering leaf that may turn brown. There is progressive dieback of branches and a purplish fungus grows on the dead wood, which may later turn white or brown. Spores enter via a wound, so never prune in winter when the cuts cannot heal. Cut out and destroy affected branches in summer and paint the wounds. Sterilise all tools after use on diseased trees.

- Heavy cropping can be a problem and wooden props may be needed to support branches that are laden with fruit, otherwise, the branches may split away from the tree.

HARVESTING THE FRUIT.

THE ALLOTMENT GARDENER

222

FIG – Ficus carica

- Perennial
- Height 3.5–4m
- Spread 3–3.5m

Figs are a delicious fruit but quite expensive to buy in the greengrocers' and it is not easy to find perfectly ripe fruit on sale. They are quite easy to grow and will produce the best crops in the south. In colder areas, pot-grown figs are easier to care for, as in winter as they can be stored indoors.

VARIETIES

Brown Turkey – for picking August-September. This is the most popular variety for outdoor growing. A hardy and reliable tree with a heavy crop of brownish purple fruit with a dark red tinge to the flesh.

Brunswick – for picking August-September. A reliable outdoor fig with larger pale green oval shaped fruit. The yields are good but lower than Brown Turkey.

White Marseilles – for picking in August. The fruit is distinctly pear-shaped, large and pale green with white juicy flesh and a rich sweet flavour. Good for growing in pots, or in milder areas.

PLANTING

Buying a plant

Look for a two-year old pot-grown plant with healthy dark green leaves. Avoid plants with yellow leaves, or those that are pot bound with a mass of roots coming out of the drainage holes.

Where to plant

Choose a sunny, sheltered, south facing spot. Positioning against a wall or fence will protect from the effects of frost. Roots need to be restricted or the tree will grow too vigorously and there will be little fruits. To restrict root growth plant in a 38cm pot or a lined pit. Figs prefer a slightly alkaline soil and if pH is less than 6, add some lime.

POT-GROWN FIG PLANT.

Planting a fig tree

- In November-March dig a trough and line it with concrete slabs. Tightly line the base with broken bricks to a depth of 23cm. If planting against a wall, position the trough 23cm away from the wall.

- Fill the trough with good loam and plant the pot-grown tree to the same level as its pot, spreading the roots well out. Firm the soil and water in well.

- If training against a wall, construct a system of wire supports 30cm apart. Tie in the branches to the wires with soft string.

- In April, mulch the newly planted tree with manure, and repeat every year.

WATERING THE PLANTS IN SUMMER IS ESSENTIAL.

IN SEASON

Spring

In March, prune away unhealthy or crowded shoots from established trees.

Summer

In June, pinch back young fruit-bearing growth to four or five leaves to encourage figs to form between branches.

Regular watering is essential, as the tree has restricted root growth. The root ball must never be allowed to dry out, particularly when the fruits are starting to swell in early summer.

Winter

Plant new trees Nov–March during the dormant season.

The embryo fruits and young shoots need to be covered in winter to protect them. Protect the next year's harvest by tying a layer of straw around the embryo figs; at the same time, remove any unripe figs from last summer.

PICKING AND STORING

Allow the fruits to ripen on the tree. They are ready for harvesting when the stalk weakens and the fully coloured fruit hangs downwards. The skin may crack and there may be a drop of nectar near the base of the fig when they are fully ripe. Gather the fruit carefully and keep in a single layer in a cool place for several weeks.

PESTS AND DISEASES

Figs grown in the open are usually pest-free, but plants grown under cover may attract whitefly. Use an insecticidal soap spray to control these.

LEAVE THE GREEN FRUITS TO RIPEN ON THE VINE.

225

GOOSEBERRY
~ Ribes uva crispa

- Perennial
- Height 1-2m
- Spread 1-1.5m

All gooseberries start out green, but depending on their variety, they can develop into a gold, yellow, purple or red colour. They come in dessert varieties, which have a sweet flavour, dual-purpose varieties that can be eaten fresh or used in cooking, and culinary varieties that are best for cooking. These delicious fruits are the first of the early summer berries and are traditionally cooked in pastry pies, tarts and crumbles. They freeze well in a single layer on trays, just after picking.

VARIETIES

Careless – crops mid-July. A popular variety, easily available. A reliable cropper with smooth, crisp berries, excellent flavour for cooking.

Invicta – crops late July. Heavy crops of large green smooth fruits. The thorny bush is mildew-resistant and has a spreading habit.

Lord Derby – crops early August. A small, compact bush with large, reddish black berries. The smooth round berries have a good flavour and high yield.

Golden Drop – crops mid July. Moderate yields of small golden yellow thin-skinned fruits with an excellent flavour for serving fresh. A good choice where space is limited as the bush is compact in growth.

PLANTING

Buying a plant
Buy bare-rooted plants with strong roots. Avoid plants with withered tips, as these will not establish well. Look for signs of powdery white mildew and avoid.

Where to plant

- Gooseberries are hardy and can generally be planted in any soil.
- Well-drained, moist, humus-rich soil is best, but digging in organic compost will create a good base.
- Choose a site in full sun if possible, but gooseberries will fruit in partial shade. Avoid exposed windy sites.

Planting a gooseberry bush

- Dig over the ground at least a month before planting, removing all weeds. Remove the top spit of soil and add a 9cm layer of garden compost in the hole. Fork in and return the soil to the hole. Scatter 50g of Growmore over the ground before planting.
- Plant the bare-rooted bushes in October-November or February-March, adding a thick layer of organic mulch around the base of each bush.

GOOSEBERRY BUSH.

BEND OVER A STEM INTO A SMALL HOLE AND BURY THE MIDDLE PORTION TO MAKE A NEW ROOTED PLANT FOR NEXT SPRING.

Raising new plants

- In spring, select a long lanky stem that you will be able to bend to the ground. Dig a shallow hole near where the end of the stem reaches the ground.
- Bend the top of the stem into the hole, letting the far end come up out of the hole. Cover the part of the stem that is in the hole with soil, then lay a small brick or stone over the buried portion.
- Next spring, check for root growth. If the stem has rooted, cut it away from the mother plant, dig up with a large root ball and replant.

IN SEASON

Spring

Spread organic mulch made from straw or rotted leaves round the bushes to suppress weeds and keep in moisture.

Summer

Water thoroughly and regularly in summer if the weather is dry. If the crop is heavy, start to thin it out in May-June, removing some of the berries, which can be used for cooking.

Winter

Cut out any stems that are more than three years old and thin out any excess shoots, leaving upright robust and disease free stems to keep the bush in a goblet shape.

PRUNING AWAY LANKY STEMS.

PICKING AND STORING

For eating fresh, leave the berries to fully ripen on the bush. When picking, run your hand under the berries – only the ripe berries will drop off into your hand. Store berries in the shade when picking.

For cooking, harvest the gooseberries while they are green, hard and under ripe but have reached their mature size.

Harvest the fruit in several pickings, as all the berries will not be ready at once. Store in a refrigerator for one–two weeks or freeze in a single layer on trays.

PESTS AND DISEASES

American gooseberry mildew leaves a white powdery mildew dust on the shoots, later becoming a brown felt over the surface. Bushes should be pruned regularly and infected shoots removed and burnt. Spray in the spring when the first flowers open.

GREENGAGE
~ Prunus italica

- Hardy tree
- Height 4–5m
- Spread 2–4m

Greengages are like small green plums with sweet, golden scented flesh. They crop in mid-summer before the main plum harvest, so make the most of these delicacies, which can be made into pies, tarts, jams and conserves.

VARIETIES

Old Green Gage – has an excellent flavour and small round green fruits. Good crops in late august.

Cambridge Gage – an old variety with yellowish green juicy fruits. Good vigorous growth and heavy cropper in southern areas but not suitable for colder northern areas.

Denniston's Superb – for picking in early August. Hardy and reliable yields and better for northern areas.

PLANTING

Buying a tree
Buy a two–three year-old partly trained tree from a reputable nursery.

Where to plant
Plant in moist but free-draining soil. Enrich poor or light soil with well-rotted compost or manure.

Planting a greengage bush
- Plant November to March when the bush is dormant. In early autumn, dig over a plot and enrich with a slow-release granular fertiliser or well-rotted manure or compost.

- Dig a hole and drive in a stake for support or plant against a wall with staked or wired supports. Plant the bush, fill in the hole with soil, firm in and water well.
- Tie to the stake or tie and train the branches to the wall wires. In March cut back the lateral branches by one half. Do not prune the central leader branch.

IN SEASON

Spring
Spray with a liquid seaweed solution or nitrogen-rich fertiliser. Protect buds from bird damage with netting.

Summer
Water regularly in dry weather.

GROWING BUSH.

Autumn
Prop up heavy fruit laden branches with wooden posts to prevent the branches from splitting

PICKING AND STORING

Make sure to pick the fruit when dry, as wet fruit will soon go mouldy. Pick ripe fruits when they pull away from the tree easily. The ripe fruits will not store well, so eat or use immediately to make jams, jellies tarts or pies.

PESTS AND DISEASES

Spray to control infestations of aphids or caterpillars. Birds will be attracted to the fruits so protect with netting or cotton threads tied across branches.

LAXTON'S GAGE FRUIT.

MULBERRY TREE – Morus spp.

- Hardy tree
- Height up to 9m
- Spread 2.5m

This beautiful tree is long-lived and produces delicious fruits with a sweet but sharp flavour. Avoid the ornamental varieties, which produce white fruits, as these can be insipid in flavour, whereas the trees bearing the deep red and darker blackish red fruits have the best flavours.

VARIETIES

Chelsea – black mulberry variety with good-sized fruits. Crops late from August–September.

Morus Rubra – for picking in August to September. This delicious fruit ripens from red into purple. Tree has bright yellow autumn foliage.

PLANTING

Buying a mulberry tree

Choose a three-five year old container-grown tree with about four shoots. Don't buy bare-rooted plants as the roots are easily damaged.

Where to plant

Position in an open sunny site. In colder or northern areas, protect with some shelter or plant by a wall. Thrives in any rich, fertile well-drained soil.

FRUIT RIPENS FROM RED TO DARK PURPLE.

Planting a mulberry tree

- Soak the root ball of the tree in water for two hours before planting.
- Dig a hole large enough to take the roots when extended. Drive a wooden stake in the hole to support the tree.
- Plant the tree to the same depth it was in the container. Spread out the roots and position 5cm away from the stake.
- Tie into the stake using a tree tie, then fill in the planting hole with soil. Firm in and water well.

IN SEASON

Spring
Scatter granular fertiliser round the base or spray with liquid seaweed solution.

Summer
Harvest fruit.

Winter
Cut back shoots and trim the tree into a good shape but keep pruning to a minimum.

HARVESTING — PLACE PLASTIC SHEET UNDER THE TREE TO CATCH THE FRUIT AS IT FALLS.

PICKING AND STORING

From late August to September pick the berries by hand or place a plastic sheet beneath the branches and collect the berries as they fall, to keep them clean. Use the berries on the day of picking or freeze immediately.

PESTS AND DISEASES

The tree is fairly disease-free, but birds will be attracted to the juicy fruits. Protect by covering young trees with netting, or tie old silver cd discs to the branches to reflect the light and scare birds away.

NECTARINES & PEACHES
~ Prunus persica

PEACHES

- Tree
- Up to 5m
- Spread up to 5m

Outdoor and dwarf varieties of peach can be grown against sheltered south-facing walls. They need warmth and a suntrap for the fruit to ripen successfully, or can be grown inside in greenhouses in colder northern climates.

VARIETIES

Peaches

Breda – a high-yielding variety, orange-red with a good flavour. Crops in early autumn.

Peregrine – for picking in early August. This is the most popular variety, with juicy flesh with a delicious flavour. High yields if positioned against an outside wall.

Rochester – yellow juicy firm flesh. Crops mid-august. Good all round variety that flowers late, missing the frosts.

Nectarines

Lord Napier – outdoor variety with firm white aromatic flesh, packed with flavour. Heavy cropper. Reliable regular crops in early August.

Hayles Early – softer fleshed fruits with a good flavour. Prolific crops in late July.

POT-GROWN PEACH TREE.

THE ALLOTMENT GARDENER

PLANTING

Buying a tree

Buy bare-rooted trees in spring and look for guaranteed stock. Select a rootstock that will grow to a size that suits your land.

Where to plant

Peaches and nectarines need the sunniest possible position to thrive. Choose a position with at least 4-6 hours of sunlight per day sheltered away from winds. Well-drained sandy soil is best to ensure good drainage.

As flowers or buds can be killed by spring frosts, cover small trees with horticultural fleece if there is danger of extreme frost.

Dwarf peach trees are ideal for smaller plots and can be trained against a wall or trellis or even grown in a large container.

Planting a tree

- Soak the roots of the tree in a bucket of water for up to 24 hours.
- If planting near a wall, position about 23cm away from the wall and slope the stem slightly inwards.
- Dig a hole twice the width and depth of the root mass. Mix one part compost to two parts soil with the soil from the hole.
- Prune away any twisted, broken or dead roots. Form a cone with the soil in the hole and spread the tree roots over the mound.
- Fill in the hole with two thirds of the soil and firm in with your hands. Water well then add the remaining soil and water again.
- To train into a fan shape, tie each branch to a cane. Tie the canes of the two main branches to wires, each at a 45-degree angle. Spread out all the remaining canes to form a well-shaped fan and tie to wires. Each February, cut about one third off of each cane, pruning back to a bud. As more canes develop, tie them into the wires in a fan shape.

IN SEASON

Spring

Prune dwarf trees into shape, removing dead wood. Cut out any weak or crossing branches.

Protect the blossom from frost with fleece or hessian sacking.

Summer

When fruit is 2cm wide, thin out leaving 15cm spaces in between each one.

COVERING A NECTARINE/PEACH TREE WITH HORTICULTURAL FLEECE TO PROTECT FROM FROSTS.

PRUNING BACK A PEACH TREE.

Winter

Plant in November for next spring's crop.

PICKING AND STORING

Harvest when the fruit is firm and ripe and has a mature colour. The fruits should come away with a gentle twist. After picking, store peaches at 15-21°C for 24 hours for the best flavour. Nectarines are ripe when they are slightly soft to the touch and have a fruity fragrance.

PESTS AND DISEASES

Peach leaf curl can cause the leaves of both nectarines and peaches to blister and swell. Leaves will turn red then white and weaken the tree. As the fungus over-winters on the bark and buds, spray in late winter with dithane.

NECTARINE

PEAR - Pyrus communis

- Tree
- Height 2-3m
- Spread 2-3m

These tasty autumn fruits can be divided into early, mid-season and late croppers. Pears store well, and one or two trees will give you plenty of fruit for cooking and eating. Since most pear trees are not self-pollinating, you will need to plant two varieties together, which will cross-pollinate to ensure a good crop. New family trees carry more than one variety on a single plant; the basic type carries Conference, Doyenne du Comice and Williams Bon Chretien.

VARIETIES

Beth – early season. Crops late August. Regular high cropping yields. Golden yellow fruits with succulent white flesh. Good for eating. Plant with Conference for pollination.

Conference – mid-season. Crops late September. Olive-green and russet fruits. Good for cooking and storing. Partly self-fertile, but pair with Comice for pollination.

Concorde – late season. Crops late October. Long narrow fruits with good flavour with very juicy flesh. Good for small plots where protection from wind is provided.

PLANTING

Buying a pear tree

Buy 2-3 year-old bare-rooted trees for winter or spring planting, and container-grown trees for planting in autumn. One year-old trees are cheaper, but will need several years of growth before they begin to fruit.

Where to plant

Dessert pears will need full sun. Some varieties will tolerate partial shade, but choose a sunny site if possible. Pear trees thrive best in well-drained, loamy soil that retains moisture, particularly during the summer months.

Planting a pear tree

- If you can position the tree against a sunny wall this provides shelter and an opportunity to fan or espalier train the branches.
- Soak the roots overnight in a tub before planting. Before spring planting, lightly prune back the top of each branch by about a third. Cut away any broken or damaged roots.
- Dig a hole twice the size of the root system. Mix compost with the soil from the hole. Place the tree in the hole at the same depth it grew in the nursery. Place a stake in the hole and refill with soil.
- Water in well and attach the tree to the stake with a soft tie, or attach to wires against a sunny wall and tie the branches into a pyramid shape.

ESPALIER OR FAN TRAINING AGAINST A WIRE TRELLIS SUPPORT.

237

IN SEASON

Spring
Prune young trees to help develop one central trunk. On older trees remove branches to let the sun into the centre for better fruit. Feed and mulch around the tree with shredded bark and water in.

Summer
If necessary, use insecticide soap to control insects.

Autumn
Place tree guards around the trunk if you have rabbits that damage the bark.

PICKING AND STORING

The fruit is ripe for picking when it parts easily from the tree when lifted in the palm of your hand and given a twist. With early varieties, fruit should be removed when fully grown but not fully ripened. If picking under-ripe pears, cut the stalks from the tree and leave the fruit for four to five days to ripen. Late varieties can be picked and ripened in storage. To store, wrap each pear in tissue paper and store in a box or wooden crate in a single layer in a cool place.

PESTS AND DISEASES

Firebright will cause blackening of leaves and will cause the tree to die eventually. Prune away affected areas and destroy the branches.

Sterilise your pruning tools after use to prevent re-infection.

OPPOSITE: PROTECT THE BARK FROM RABBIT DAMAGE BY WRAPPING A WIRE TREE GUARD ROUND THE BARK.

TOP: MULCHING THE ROOTS OF A NEW PEAR TREE WITH SHREDDED BARK GIVES IT A GOOD START.

RIGHT: CONFERENCE PEARS.

PLUMS & GAGES
~ Prunus domestica

- Perennial
- Height 2-6m
- Spread 2-4m

These sweet juicy fruit are so popular; they can be divided into dessert plums, culinary plums for cooking, and gages. They are easy to grow in most areas but as they flower in spring, late frosts may destroy blossom in colder areas. Fan-trained plum trees positioned against a south-facing wall will give good crops. Cross-pollination is not essential for most varieties, but more fruit may be produced when a plum tree is planted next to another variety.

VARIETIES

Czar – early cropper – August. Self-fertile and frost-resistant. Oval, purple, medium-sized fruits good for cooking. Reliable heavy cropper

Opal – early cropper – late July. Heavy crops of dark red, juicy plums.

Victoria – mid-season cropper – early September. Popular, reliable plum with heavy crops and a good flavour for cooking.

Cambridge Gage – mid season cropper – late August. Small round yellow green fruits with a good flavour and regular crop.

THE ALLOTMENT GARDENER

Marjorie's Seedling – late season cropper – late September. Oval purple fruits with yellow flesh. Reliable heavy crops. Self-fertile.

Edwards – late season cropper – September. Large blue fruits with creamy white flesh. Good for desserts, stewing and bottling.

PLANTING

Buying a plum tree

In autumn, buy bare-rooted trees at least two years old as trees less than two years old will not bear fruit for several years. Look for dwarfing rootstock such as 'Pixy' and avoid trees with dry woody roots.

Where to plant

Choose a high spot in an open site that gets lots of sun. Make sure there is plenty of space for the tree to grow and the air to circulate around it. Avoid planting where soil is damp.

Planting a plum tree

- Before planting, soak the roots in a tub of water overnight.
- Dig a hole twice as large as the root ball. Mix one part compost to two parts soil and add a handful of general-purpose fertiliser.
- Plant the tree in the hole to the same depth it grew in the nursery. Fill the hole with soil and water the tree, soaking thoroughly.
- Next spring, cut back the branches by one third. Mulch with shredded bark around the base of the tree.

VICTORIA PLUMS.

IN SEASON

Spring

In June remove any dead, diseased or broken branches. Keep pruning to a minimum to reduce overcrowded branches. Feed and mulch.

Summer

In early summer when plums are the size of marbles, thin out the fruit to about 5cm apart to help produce large high quality fruit.

Autumn

Protect ripening fruit from birds with netting, silver cd discs or small empty plastic bottles that will clatter and make a noise. Prop up any branches overloaded with fruit, so that they do not tear away from the tree.

PROTECT RIPENING FRUIT FROM DAMAGE FROM BIRDS BY TYING ON OLD CD COMPUTER DISKS

HARVEST FRUIT WHEN IT IS SLIGHTLY SOFT TO THE TOUCH.
TWIST THE FRUIT AWAY FROM THE BRANCH WITH AN UPWARD MOTION

PICKING AND STORING

Plums are ripe when they pull easily from the tree. To avoid bruising the fruit, pick the fruit with an upward twisting movement, leaving the stalk on the branch. Culinary varieties should be picked while the fruit is still unripe. Dessert plums will keep for a few days if ripe. If picked slightly unripe they will store for one–two weeks in a cool place.

PESTS AND DISEASES

Silver leaf is a serious disease that affects the plum tree. Spores enter via wounds so do not prune in winter when cuts cannot heal. Cut away and destroy any affected branches in spring.

QUINCE
– Cydonia oblongata

- Perennial
- Height 4m
- Spread 3–4m

Quinces trees are long-lived and are covered in glorious yellow foliage in autumn. The small bushy trees produce rare fruits with an aromatic flavour and gritty texture. The fruits cannot be eaten raw but make delicious jellies or can be added to apple pies and desserts for a zesty fresh flavour.

VARIETIES

Vranja (Bereczki) – from Serbia produces large pear shaped fruits, with good flavour. The tree had good erect growth and crops early.

Meech's Prolific – pale yellow pear-shaped fruits with an excellent flavour. Slow-growing but early to bear fruit. Crops are heavy and regular and are good for winter storage.

Champion – large round apple-shaped fruits with a delicate mild flavour. Trees bear fruit when young.

PLANTING

Buying a quince tree
Look for a two–three year-old grafted tree with about six branches.

Where to plant
Position in a sheltered spot in full sun avoiding frost hollows. Plant in deep moist soil.

Planting a quince tree

- Plant container-grown trees from November to March. Dig a wide hole deep enough to spread out the roots when fully extended and scatter in a handful of general purpose slow-release fertiliser.
- Drive in a stake for support. Place the tree in the hole and spread out the roots. Fill the hole with soil, firm in and water well. Attach the trunk to the stake.
- Prune back all main branches by one third to an outward facing bud.

IN SEASON

Spring

Spray with liquid seaweed solution every month. Mulch round the base with compost to keep down weeds and retain moisture.

QUINCE TREE.

Summer

Continue to spray with liquid seaweed solution every month.

Winter

After harvesting, prune away last year's growth and any dead wood.

YELLOW FRUITS ON THE TREE — LEAVE AS LATE AS POSSIBLE TO DEVELOP THE FLAVOUR.

PICKING AND STORING

Leave the fruits on the tree as late as possible until yellow, to develop the flavour, but pick before frosts set in from October-November. Store the yellow, ripe fruits in one layer in a wooden tray. Do not store near apples or pears, as the strong perfume will taint other fruits.

PESTS AND DISEASES

Quince trees are relatively trouble-free, but late spring frosts may damage flowers and subsequent crops. Planting in a warm sunny spot near a wall will give extra protection. Leaf-eating caterpillars can attack in spring and spraying with a systemic insecticide will help.

HARVESTING

RASPBERRY
~ Rubus iadaeus

- Perennial
- Height 1.5-3m
- Spread 1.25-3m

Raspberry plants need very little care and provide a wonderful harvest of succulent juicy fruits. There are two types of raspberry: summer, and autumn-fruiting.

VARIETIES

Malling Admiral – summer-fruiting. Crops July-August. Good flavoured berries with a high yield. Pest resistant and thornless.

Leo – summer-fruiting. Crops August. Tangy flavour and good firm fruit. Disease-resistant. Vigorous growth.

Autumn Bliss – autumn-fruiting, crops August-October. Good flavoured fruit and high yield. Strong plants do no require support.

Heritage – autumn-fruiting. Crops September-October. Strong-growing, hardy bush. Good flavoured firm berries.

PLANTING

Buying a plant
Buy certified disease-resistant plants with strong canes. Look for plants with no leaf growth. Avoid those that look dried-out.

Where to plant

Raspberries do best in mild areas. Plant in full sun, preferably a sheltered east-facing location. The plants need good drainage and rich, deep well manured soil.

Planting raspberry canes

- Before planting, soak the roots in water for two hours and cut back any damaged roots.
- Double dig a trench and mix 8-10cm compost in the base. Plant the roots only, spreading them out to encourage suckers. Cover and firm in, then water well.
- Prune the newly planted stems to a bud 30cm above the ground. Tie in to wire supports tied to a post.

IN SEASON

Spring

Apply a general fertiliser in March and mulch with well-rotted manure.

Summer

Cut back canes of summer-fruiting varieties to the ground after harvesting. Water well in dry weather. Cover with netting when first in flower to protect, and then remove as necessary to harvest the crop.

Autumn

Pull off unwanted suckers and cut away the weakest canes. Leave the best six–nine canes and tie to wires 8-10cm apart.

Winter

Cut autumn-fruiting bushes down to the ground in February.

CUTTING CANES BACK TO GROUND LEVEL AFTER FRUITING.

PICKING AND STORING

Pick fruit on a dry day and pick only berries that pull easily away from the core. Pick every day, as the berries will rot easily after they ripen. Firm dry berries will keep for four–five days in a single layer on a tray in the fridge. Open freeze berries on trays if you have a glut of fruit.

PESTS AND DISEASES

Raspberry beetles are a pest as the white grubs feed inside the fruit and can only be seen when the fruit is picked. Spray with malathion until fruit first turns pink.

WHITE RASPBERRY.

PICKING RASPBERRIES — CHOOSE THE ONES THAT EASILY PULL OFF THE CORE.

STRAWBERRY
~ Fragaria

- Perennial
- Height 15-25cm
- Spread 20-40cm

Strawberries are the most delicious fruit and they are easy to grow in a corner of your vegetable plot or garden. If you plant different types of strawberries you can have a good supply all summer long. There are three kinds of strawberries: summer-fruiting, perpetual and alpine. Summer-fruiting varieties are some of the tastiest, flower in spring, then bear one crop in early summer. Perpetual varieties flower and bear fruit in small flushes in spring and summer, but the main crop is in autumn. The alpine strawberry is a form of a wild mountain strawberry with a tiny delicious aromatic fruit, much prized by gourmet cooks.

VARIETIES

Cambridge Favourite – summer-fruiting variety for picking June-July. A good reliable crop, which keeps well.

Elvira – summer-fruiting variety for picking in June. A heavy cropper with good flavour. The conical fruits are large but mildew can be a problem. Recommended for growing under cloches.

Tamella – perpetual variety for picking mid-June-July. High yields and a long productive life. Medium-flavoured berries crop over a long season. A good choice for colder northern counties.

Aromel – perpetual variety for picking in September. Irregular shaped berries, whose flavour is outstanding, but the crop can be moderate.

Baron Solemacher – alpine variety for picking June-October. The most popular alpine variety and can be grown in partial shade.

Alexandria – alpine variety for picking July-October. The largest alpine with excellent juicy fruit and flavour. The plant has no runners.

PLANTING

Buying a plant
Buy guaranteed disease-free plants, either bare-rooted or pot-grown. Look for plants with broad leaves and well developed roots. Avoid those that look dried out or have distorted leaves.

Where to plant
Perpetual and summer-fruiting strawberries prefer full sun. Alpines grow best in partial shade. All varieties need well-drained soil. They will thrive in raised beds and most soil, but avoid planting in heavy clay.

Planting a strawberry bed
- Dig the soil over a month before planting, removing all weeds. Mix in compost or well-rotted manure and scatter 50g general fertiliser such as Growmore over the ground just before planting.
- Soak bare-rooted plants for two hours before planting and trim away any damaged or dead leaves.
- Make a hole and round up the soil in the centre. Spread the roots over the mound and plant with the central buds above the soil. Space the plants 45cm apart in rows 75cm apart. Mulch with clean straw and keep the plants well watered.

MULCHING WITH CLEAN STRAW.

- Planting through 150 gauge black polythene sheeting helps protect the fruit from slugs and soil. Lay black plastic over a raised bed and tuck the edges into the soil in order to retain moisture and keep the bed weed free. Cut slits in the plastic large enough for the plants.

PLANTING THROUGH BLACK PLASTIC.

IN SEASON

Spring

Plant pot-grown plants after the frosts, when the soil warms up.

Summer

In new plants, allow each strawberry to grow only four–five runners and remove the rest. Pinch off runners for a small yield and large fruit, but for a heavy yield and smaller fruit, let the runners grow.

PICKING AND STORING

Choose dry weather and harvest when the berries are dry and have a full red colour. Try to avoid bruising the fruit. Pinch the fruits away leaving the green stems and outer whorls intact.

PESTS AND DISEASES

Botrytis, a grey mould, spreads rapidly in wet weather. Destroy any diseased fruit, then spray with a fungicide.

Aphids will weaken and damage the plants and spread virus disease. Spray with an eco friendly pesticide such as Pirmicarb, that will kill aphids and not bees.

OPPOSITE: A SPECIALLY DESIGNED STRAWBERRY POT WILL GIVE A GOOD CROP.
LEFT: STRAWBERRY PLANT AND FRUIT.

INDEX

THE ALLOTMENT GARDENER

credits &
acknowledgements

The author and publishers would like to thank the following people for their help in creating this book:

Laura Forrester for the photography, and her able assistant Stephen Ambrose.

Brian Taylor of the Sidegate Lane Allotments for letting us use his allotment and for all his gardening help and advice.